King Con

The Story of Soapy Smith

Jane G. Haigh

King Con: The Story of Soapy Smith
by Jane G. Haigh

ISBN 0-9780367-0-0

Cover Photograph: Jeff Smith as he appeared in Denver in the 1890s.
(Denver Public Library F17094)
Editor: Ann Chandonnet
Copy Editor: Colleen Anderson and Nina Mollett
Design and Production: Friday 501 Media Ltd.
Printed and bound in China

We acknowledge the financial support of the Government of Canada through the Book Publishing Industry Development Program (BPIDP) for our publishing activities.

For Chris, Anna and Molly who have always humored me by feigning interest.
J.G.H.

FRIDAY 501

Box 31599, Whitehorse, Yukon, Y1A 6L2
867-668-668-3501, Fax 867-668-4472
www.friday501.com, info@friday501.com

Contents

Preface

Alaskans and visitors know Jefferson Randolph "Soapy" Smith (1860-1898) as the con man who took over Skagway at the height of the Klondike Gold Rush. His colorful reign lasted less than one short year, and most of what we think we know is based on oft-repeated local anecdotes synthesized from period rumors. Because so little is known beyond the colorful stories, Soapy's problematic personality has become the central focus of the legend, dramatized every summer for more than seventy-five years in Skagway's amusing and dramatic "Days of '98 Show." Many Alaskans consider Soapy an enigmatic figure and question whether there were not, after all, some redeeming qualities to his nature.

My editors Graham Wilson and John Small, piqued my interest in Soapy Smith when they mentioned that that there was no good book in print about the most famous bad guy in Alaskan history, the victim of a true Wild West-style shoot-out on Skagway's wharf in July 1898. As I looked further into the subject, I was soon utterly fascinated.

The big question seemed to be, how could one man take over a whole town? It couldn't have happened spontaneously; Soapy must have had a plan. And from the descriptions of the fake telegraph office and information bureau, which, as far as contemporaneous Skagway observers were concerned, seemingly sprang to life overnight, there were many individuals involved. Could one man have invented so many swindles and organized the participants on the spot? The evidence seemed to add up to a substantial organization with experience in the operation of these scams before they arrived in the North. Then there was a second big question: Why did the people of Skagway not try to rid themselves of the slippery Soapy and his larcenous gang sooner, and why did many aid and abet his cause?

My third and final question: What caused Smith, with all his talents and gifts, to take the low road as Soapy instead of using his talents in a more constructive forum? Descended from a well-off family in Georgia, whose uncles and cousins were lawyers, ministers, and businessmen, Jeff Smith himself was by all accounts a personable, gifted speaker well versed in the social arts that were prized in the Victorian nineteenth century. He was kind to children and poor people, a good father, and, in Skagway, acted the part of a benevolent, churchgoing community member when he was not coaching and protecting the criminal element.

The two most comprehensive biographies of Soapy were written in 1937 and 1961; both published in Denver, where as it turns out, Soapy earned his famous moniker and learned everything he knew about the con games that in the nineteenth century were called bunco. In search of Soapy's past, I traveled to Denver, where the *Denver Public Library* proved to be my own modern gold mine as a historian of the nineteenth century West. Soapy was a familiar figure and noted bad actor in Denver for almost twenty years. Denver in fact, turns out to have been a true school for scandal, "Con Man U," run by Soapy's personal mentor, "Doc" Charles Baggs. My investigations into Soapy and his activities led me to a treasure trove of information on the bunco men and their gangs, and their political ties, a topic so fascinating that it will be the subject of my dissertation.

In this book, the first complete biography in over forty years, I have put together the story of Soapy Smith in all its frontier and boomtown glory, and tried to answer the questions it raises. My original research has led to the conclusion that Soapy and his gang indeed arrived with the intention of controlling the unformed town on Skagway Bay, a fact largely missing from the understanding of the story in Skagway. What this King of Cons accomplished employed a plan that he had been developing for probably ten years, had tried out in Creede, Colorado six years previously, and had then been waiting for the right opportunity to put it into play again. It was like a complex Civil War battle plan that had existed only on paper, and had now sprung to life.

Soapy learned all he knew about the art of the bunco game from the confidence fraternity's elder statesmen during his time in Denver, where the bunco and con games they played had all been invented and perfected on street corners, in saloons and in Big Stores, the fronts for duping the would-be innocent. The gang they assembled, and which Soapy arose in the ranks to head, was a loose conglomeration of individuals, many of whom had already been associates for years.

The clever cons and their bunco games exploited the Victorian focus on social class, and especially exploited the markers of middle-class status such as deportment, elocution, dress, and grooming. They subverted this system to prey on the very people who most relied on the visual symbols of social classes at a time, the end of the 19th century, and a place, the West, when these symbols and the social classes they served to distinguish were at their most fluid.

Soapy's best defense was his use of obfuscation: purposely spreading disinformation to create confusion. For many of the people who lived through that cold, foggy winter of 1897-98 in Skagway, the whole drama unfolded like the plot of a convoluted mystery novel. No one who was there at the time could really have been aware of all that was going on. Everyone involved from children to bankers to deputies to hotel keepers had their own views of events, their own rationalizations, and, often, their own personal falsehoods. (The chaos of the Klondike Gold Rush gave hundreds of people the opportunity to leave disreputable former lives and, often, former names behind. Ma Pullen, for example, who claimed to be a widow, still had a husband living outside Alaska. Frank Reid, the city engineer, was not quite the innocent he seemed.) Sorting fact from fiction in the story of Soapy and Skagway has presented one of the biggest difficulties in deciding what facts to use here. (See Note on Sources below.)

The story here is as I have now come to understand it. I will not further confuse the issue by presenting all of the other versions of events—particularly the versions of the final duel on the Juneau Company wharf.

Note on Sources

For Soapy's early life, and his exploits in Colorado, I have relied first on the two previous biographies, Robertson and Harris's *Soapy Smith: King of the Frontier Con Men*, and Collier and Westrate's *The Reign of Soapy Smith, Monarch of Misrule*. Biographies and autobiographies of Soapy's contemporaries, early books and various collections at both the Denver Public Library and the Colorado Historical Society, and in the pages of the *Rocky Mountain News*, as well as other newspapers and magazines helped complete a picture of Soapy's exploits.

Sorting out fact from fiction, information from misinformation about Soapy's months in Skagway has been one of the biggest difficulties. Primary sources are not necessarily factual. For example, *Skaguay News* publisher and editor M. L. Sherpy was a major Skagway booster, and a supporter of Soapy's gang. Sherpy railed continually against "disloyalty to Skaguay." His advice: "Brace up and tell everyone you meet that you know Skaguay is bound to be the metropolis of Alaska and you will soon believe it yourself." He did all he could to leave Soapy, his swindling actions or the robberies, muggings, and murders committed by those complicit with him, out of the news. Some of his major advertisers were known gang members; W. F. Saportas is mentioned in every issue. Furthermore, the paper did not publish its first edition until October, and many of the numbers of this first year and the next are missing. So, though the incident of the bartender, Fay, murdering Rowan and McGrath is a key event, it is barely mentioned in the *Skaguay News*. Nevertheless, the paper and its reporters such as "Stroller" White were reporting firsthand, on-the-spot information, as opposed to the Seattle papers, which, since there was no telegraph, relied on interviews with whomever happened to be disembarking at the Seattle waterfront, interviews that were conducted at least five days after leaving Skagway. Not all of these incidental witnesses had the facts straight.

So, according to articles in the Seattle papers, this one shooting incident is supposed to have taken place in the *Klondike Saloon* operated by Jake Rice. In fact, Jake Rice operated the *Peoples Theater*. The *Klondike Saloon*, which moved from Trail to Holly Street in November 1897, was operated by Coslet and Word. Both the theater and the *Klondike Saloon* were advertised as being at the corner of Holly and Trail, but was the saloon above the theater, next door, separate, or the same establishment? *The Klondike* is mentioned so often in the miscellaneous text section of Sherpy's paper that it seems reasonable to suspect that Rice was also complicit with the gang. And, of course, *Jeff Smith's Parlor* was located on Holly Street.

Only careful reading and close comparison of each story's versions, taking into account the limitations of each source, can yield the most probable description of the truth. With no formal court system or legal establishment in Skagway itself, court transcripts refer to proceedings that had occurred many months later, if at all. Furthermore, many commonplace stories about Soapy are misinforming or apocryphal; that is, common frontier stories transposed to relate to Soapy. For instance, tales of Soapy's raising funds in his saloon for an itinerant preacher or church are told in Denver, Creede, and in Skagway, and many another boomtowns as well. Oft repeated, they might have happened once, or a thousand times, but I have chosen to leave them out, as they cannot be verified in any way.

In my work on other pioneer characters, such as Doc Baggs, I have been able to use the local newspaper reports of their arrivals and hotel stays to track their whereabouts at any particular time. But Soapy did all he could to disguise and cover up his activities and his travels. He routinely used false names when traveling, and in fact, others used his name in efforts to confuse the authorities. Thus, trying to track him in passenger lists can be pointless. His comings and goings are likewise rarely mentioned. Soapy's gang was not a coherent entity with membership cards, and the illegal shenanigans that went on in Skagway were not confined to the gang.

Jeff Smith's Skagway

Fall, 1897.
Jefferson Randolph Smith strutted down Broadway to Captain Billy Moore's wharf with his head held high. He sniffed the fresh sea breeze off the shallow tide flats of Skagway Bay appreciatively. How sweet it was that after all his suffering and tribulations, after his years of wandering, the good Lord had made Skagway just for him. In this lawless town of anxious, down-at-the-heels prospectors, Smith's dapper figure could not fail to catch the eye. Although he was of average height, his upright military bearing and brimming self-confidence made him seem taller. His signature black sombrero, highly polished boots, and carefully brushed black suit set off his dark hair and dark, trimmed beard.

Since gold had been discovered in August of 1896 in the remote Klondike Valley of the Yukon, wild stories circulated that in the Klondike mining district you could pick up a fortune in gold nuggets right off the ground, if you could get there. The lure of nearly instant riches galvanized men and women alike. Newspapers and hastily printed guidebooks were calling Skagway "Gateway to the Klondike." But the words "Dawson City" were often said in the same sentence with the phrase "fifteen hundred miles from nowhere." And few knew precisely where the Klondike was. Was it in Alaska or Canada?

Thousands of men and women were mortgaging farms, retrieving hard-earned dollars from beneath mattresses, and borrowing from friends and relatives to assemble grubstakes for the difficult trip. There were only a few trails into the interior, and one of them, the White Pass, was guarded by the seaside town of Skagway. Thousands of gold seekers were due to descend on the town at the end of a deep northern fjord. And yet Congress and the President in their wisdom had not provided for any means of establishing a civic government.

Jeff was thankful for their ignorance. "Bless the leaders of our great country, Good Lord," he thought as he stooped to pat the head of a child playing in a mud puddle. For it could be only through the will of the Lord himself that he had arrived in this con man's earthly Mecca.

The summit of the Chilkoot Pass out of Dyea was so steep that sleds could not be pulled over it by man or beast. After reaching Dyea by crowded steamship, would-be prospectors had to muscle their ponderous outfits one load at a time—fifteen or more trips hauling hundred-pound packs over the rugged pass. Even the hardy Tlingit packers who were familiar with the thirty-two-mile route needed to wear snowshoes going over in the winter.

The White Pass out of Skagway was nearly five hundred feet lower and its trail less steep, allowing sleds, horses, and freight wagons along its length. But still the White Pass was so brutal that it was already known as the Dead Horse Trail. It would kill three thousand horses in its first year. And yet few of the thousands of city slickers and tenderfeet who would attempt it had any idea of the hardships that lay ahead. Truth be told, most of them were so inexperienced in the ways of wilderness that they had never even camped out. The two-month trip over a snowbound pass and down the Yukon would turn many of them back and kill others.

"Praise be to the Good Lord," said Jeff Smith out loud to himself and anyone else who might be listening, "who has seen fit to lead me here, with my followers to perform His work: saving naïve eager gold seekers from further trials and tribulation."

By the grace of Soapy Smith's dubious ministries, eager gold seekers were parted from the money they had saved and borrowed to get to the Klondike. Released from the grasp of Gold Fever or "Klondicitis," they were then free to return to the bosoms of their loved ones far away.

At least, that's how Soapy claimed to see it. To his detractors, to anyone who dared to doubt the charity of his mercenary motives, Soapy would declare in lofty tones:

> *Infinitely better that a man who is such an infant as to try to beat a man at his own game should lose money here at the seaport, than he should get into the inhospitable Arctic where such an idiot would lose it anyway, and there become a burden on the community.*

No one dared to confront him about his pronouncements or his shady operations because he surrounded himself with heavies who had gained experience in places such as San Francisco's Chinatown and the unsafe streets of Port Townsend.

To Soapy's delight, his well-oiled organization was already working like clockwork. Schemes that the gang had only dreamed about late at night in the saloons of Denver were realities here. They raked in the cash and glittering nuggets and dust, all stashed away at Jeff's Place, a saloon in a tiny, converted bank building. And news of their success was attracting more gang members every week. Some of these toughs and shills had worked with him before. Others came from Skid Road in Seattle and the Barbary Coast in San Francisco; from Pocatello and Spokane; Ft. Worth, and Butte. All of the efforts of these recruits could only increase Soapy's personal profits.

Skagway itself was chaos. Only one dock had been completed so far, and most of the gold seekers and their tons of goods were dumped on the beach. If they could not pack them quickly to higher ground, the inexorable high tides would soon swamp them, ruining sacks of sugar and flour, bacon and beans and perishable supplies beyond redemption. Beyond the beach, the main street, optimistically named Broadway, was a sea of mud. The businesses lining each side were chiefly saloons and crude hotels, still housed in tents. Billy Moore's sawmill could not keep up with the demand for lumber. And now, hordes of gold seekers were disembarking every day. Heavy snow falling on the summit of White Pass was threatening to close the trail, making all of the new arrivals Soapy's unwilling but welcome hostages for the winter.

In the confusion that was boomtown Skagway, newly arrived gold seekers needed beds, meals, horses or packers, and information. Gang members posing as dependable business leaders, guileless churchmen, wizened but knowledgeable prospectors, fellow fresh-off-the-boat cheechakos, and sympathetic public-spirited citizens were there to help. Steerers were there to befriend anxious new arrivals, gain their confidence, and direct them to various gang enterprises: the *Telegraph Agency*, *Reliable Packers*, the *Information Bureau*, *Merchants Exchange*, *Cut-Rate Ticket Office*, and other spurious businesses that mysteriously appeared and disappeared during the next ten months. Although each business boasted its own convincingly furnished office and solicitous staff, all were merely spurious fronts, entirely fictitious enterprises.

Down at the beach, another steamer from Seattle was disgorging its cargo in ragged piles. Horses hitched to wagons worked up to their bellies in seawater. Overloaded skiffs were hastily poled to shore. And there was Slim Jim Foster, looking the part of a young but experienced fellow prospector. Foster easily befriended a promising newcomer, concerned about his myriad bags and boxes. Seeming to appear from nowhere, Foster helped the mark move his goods up the beach, chatted amiably, and soon steered him to Reliable Packers. The stranger felt fortunate to have the assistance of an experienced frontier hand, someone who knew his way around this raw new town in the wilderness. Everything seemed to be on the up and up until the stranger produced his wallet to make the small down payment to reserve the packers' services.

Suddenly, two toughs "broke in," attacked the stranger, and stole his wallet. The employees and Slim Jim, the steerer, were of course, "horrified," and made a grand show of trying to fight off the intruders. But, in the ensuing fight, somehow, the thieves got away. While the employees were sympathetic, another mark was "out-of-luck." And the "thieves" were at Jeff's snug headquarters, faithfully handing over the take, to be split among the gang.[1] Meanwhile, up on the White Pass Trail, there had been an accident: a heavily laden packhorse had fallen, blocking the trail. A lone shell game artist just happened to be on the trail behind. What to do but set up the props of his trade, the tripe and keister—or tripod and sample case? The spieler expertly manipulated the three walnut shells, daring the impatient travelers to guess which one sheltered the elusive pea. Bored as they were at the delay on the trail, most people resolved to ignore the proceedings, until another hapless and naïve traveler got sucked into the drama. And what a sapsucker he looked, a real hayseed as anyone could see. But wonder of wonders, the hayseed guessed right. The shell game artist nearly folded up his sample case table in disgust, until begged by the gathering throng to continue so they, too, could try their luck.

Thus the play gained momentum, until a sizeable amount of money had changed hands. Finally, after some delay, the horse regained its feet, the trail was cleared, and travelers continued on their way up the trail. Only after they were all out of sight did the "packers" and shell game artist and shills turn around and return to Skagway together to deposit their day's earnings at headquarters, known as *Jeff's Parlor*. Gang members carrying packs stuffed with feathers would repeat the whole drama nearly every day.

Were the bigger catches escaping Soapy's nefarious clutches? Hardly. Gang members booked passage on all the northbound ships and sized up as potential "marks" anyone who seemed prosperous, and perhaps naïve enough to have displayed a hefty bank roll, or bragged that he had enough money to hire packers for all his goods. When a ship docked, another of Soapy's men was there to greet it, acting the part of a reporter. His assignment was to interview all the arrivals who looked like they were worth plundering, and ascertain just how much money they had. While pre-identified "marks" were experiencing difficulties in the businesses operated by the gangs, other cheechakos could often be steered toward the shell game on the nearest corner, or into crooked games at Jeff Smith's fifteen-by-fifty-foot Parlor. Yes, thought Jeff, with some satisfaction, everything was proceeding according to plan.

★ ★ ★ ★

Jefferson Randolph Smith was an enigma, a puzzle of a man. Well educated, well spoken, and well dressed, he was disarming in his personal characteristics, and more difficult to classify than an ordinary back-alley murderer or thug. He was not interested in acting the part of a trail-worn bandit, cowboy train robber, or bad man, or in disguising himself as his mentor "Doc" Baggs did, as a sedate minister in tall silk hat, Prince Albert coat, white tie, and black gloves. Instead, he affected an air of suave sophistication. In an era that judged class identity according to dress, speech patterns, vocabulary, and behavior, Soapy was always dapper and well groomed. He spoke with the eloquence of an orator and tipped his hat to the ladies, all to confuse, consciously cultivating a deceptive identity. He had studied his art and risen through the ranks of western shell game artists, bunco practitioners, and con men until he came to be one of their acknowledged leaders.

In Soapy's gang, there was a place for everyone, according to his talents.[2] Spies for the gang traveled on every ship headed north from Seattle or San Francisco, identifying the affluent. Runners met the ships, debriefed the spies and planned elaborate ruses to snare the marked men. Steerers on the street conducted men uptown to the gang's various enterprises. Shell game artists conducted their games on the streets, with their cappers or ropers pulling in business. Other gang members operated the games of chance in the various saloons. Actually, "games of chance" was a euphemism, because there was virtually no chance that a sucker would win. In fact, Soapy is credited with coining the phrase "sure-thing." He is reputed to have said that he was never a gambler because he only bet on a sure thing. And of course, covering his back or at another table close by were the requisite heavies who would not hesitate to break a man's skull, or shoot him at close range, if there were any protests about the gang's methods.

The *Telegraph Agency* was a perfect example of the lengths to which the gang would go to fleece unsuspecting prospectors. The operation was equal parts audacity and acting. The office layout and accoutrements perfectly mimicked an actual agency, banked by a sign promising, "Wires to Anywhere in the U.S., $5." Inside, the gang members with their white collarless shirts, sleeve garters, and green eyeshades convincingly played their parts as telegraph operators, taking down and sending messages. In fact there was no telegraph line connecting Skagway to the world outside. The line from the "Agency" ran down into the bay and ended. Nevertheless, verisimilitude reigned. In a matter of minutes, suckers would frequently receive an answering message from a desperate wife or mother, and of course be induced to "wire money." Thus they would be bilked twice.

The brightest gang members worked the elaborate confidence or bunco games. These were intricately planned and scripted sting operations designed to fleece the well-heeled marks identified by Soapy's ring of spies. The Rev. Bowers, posing as a fellow lodge member, Syd Dixon, a disbarred lawyer, posing as a "businessman," or George Wilder, the group's suave money manager, might greet the mark. The steerer would address the stranger cordially. Apparently with the best of intentions and regard for the stranger's welfare, he would inveigle him into one of Soapy's games. Many started in *Jeff Smith's Parlor*, equipped with rigged games of chance of all sorts. "It looked innocent enough," reported the *Skagway Alaskan*, "with its polished mahogany bar, its fretwork screens, and its artificial palm trees." But even Smith's Parlor was not the intended destination for the truly wealthy. They might be inveigled into an exclusive club room in a hotel where a sky's-the-limit poker game was in progress. Unknown to the mark, however, all the other players at the table were gang members intent on only one thing: defrauding the sucker.

If the mark tried to complain to the authorities, he would find that the participants had mysteriously disappeared. Moreover, the Marshal might be only vaguely interested, and then inform the poor sucker that if indeed charges could brought, he would have to remain in Skagway for months until the case came up in court. Naturally, there were rarely any arrests.

Soapy's duties as the gang's kingpin included bribing and negotiating with officials, and hiring lawyers to defend his men when necessary. In short order, Marshal Taylor was firmly in Soapy's pocket, so that if one of the gang did get in trouble and was jailed, he usually managed to escape. The editor and publisher of the weekly newspaper *Skaguay News*, M. L. Sherpy, widely believed to be in Soapy's pay, spread the news of Soapy's good works. Throughout the winter, Sherpy led the charge, railing against any other newspaper that dared to besmirch Skagway's reputation by questioning the goings on. Soapy personally avoided the trail, and denied any knowledge of the evils occurring on it. He praised the generosity of the saloon owners and gamblers.

With his con games running smoothly, Soapy was free to concentrate on his image as a philanthropist. He acted the part of a friend of law and order and general community do-gooder. He supported churches, took in stray dogs, and encouraged civic-minded enterprises. And, after a man had lost all his money at one of the games, or been robbed, or induced to part with his outfit, a sympathetic soul or perhaps a friendly bartender would suggest that he talk to the kindly Jeff Smith.

Soapy loved to play the magnanimous benefactor. When the friendless, frantic and desperate traveler appealed for funds to rejoin the wife and kids, Jeff Smith opened his safe, and the traveler perhaps caught a glimpse of all the wallets and gold dust pokes fleeced in Skagway as Jeff counted out just enough money to pay for his passage home.

How are You Fixed for Soap?

Barely out of his teens in the spring of 1879, Jeff Smith, arrived in Denver, a young Colorado city in the vast new world of the West.[3] Quick with his hands, and with a smooth come-on patter, he was already accomplished at the art of the shell game, and more importantly, a new scam, called the soap game.

A contemporary, W. P. Carstenphen remembered Soapy's performances at the corner of 17th and Larimer. Forty years later, when the legend of Soapy Smith was still actively making the rounds, Carstenphen described the performance in a letter to the Editor of *The Trail* magazine. "Cowboys and miners thronged to Denver for the excitement and entertainment with little to do but loaf," wrote Carstenphen. "Soapy presented an excellent show with his sleight of hand performance, and always attracted a crowd, often 200 or 300. The show went on for two or three hours, and he took in sometimes $200-300."[4]

Another contemporary, George Buffam, also remembered seeing Jeff Smith on the streets of Denver in 1879:

> *Standing in front of the old Grand Central Hotel in Denver one day, I saw approaching me a man driving a bay horse hitched to a light buggy. He stopped by my side and lifted a box from the bottom of the buggy to the seat, and I noticed that it contained several cakes of soap. Looking me squarely in the face he said, "Will you allow me to present you with fifty dollars?" I declined with thanks though such benevolence might have received more consideration had I been familiar with his game.*

Buffam's account, published in 1906, is undoubtedly the earliest account of Soapy's famous spiel.[5]

> *Hear ye, Hear ye! Come gather round me, fellow citizens and rejoice for I am going to invite you to a feast where money is served with every course. This morning it will be my pleasure to distribute several hundred dollars among those who gather here. I have more cash than I have any use for. I am no money fiend who wants to pile up gold to see the eagles*

> *gather. My soap is a universal blessing and my untarnished name is its heritage. It will cleanse your consciences; it will relieve you of life's burdens. It's more than meat and drink. In my scheme of the brotherhood of man, I have a profit-sharing department. It's my business to sell soap; but listen: what do you find inside the wrappers? Perhaps it will be a hundred-dollar bill; perhaps it'll be a fifty, possible a twenty or a ten. And if by chance you don't get the currency, why, you've got a good honest soap that will brighten all the days of your life. Yesterday was a day of large profits, and this morning I must divide liberally with my fellowmen. I cannot stop to teach you how to play both ends, the top and the bottom and the sides of every cake of soap, so as to land the greenbacks every trip; but if your eye is keen and your brain alert, you will buy the cake wrapped in money, while if you are slow and stupid you will at least secure a valuable soap. That will let you ride its lather over the tallest ranges of the Rockies and through the deepest mines and if you don't stake the richest claims, it won't be my soap's fault.*
>
> *You may not win at faro; the roulette wheel may disappoint you; poker be your undoing; the race-track drive you to suicide; but my soap will float you over the sorrows and troubles of life and land you in the Elysian fields of perfect bliss....*

In Buffam's account, the spiel continues for another page or two before he describes Soapy's actions:

> *He would pick up one cake after another and seemingly place the bills inside the wrappers and put them back in the box in a most innocent and open way, as if he were anxious the watchers should select the packages containing the prizes. "How much am I offered for this cake of soap?"*
>
> *The bidding began between two of Soapy's cappers, with the successful partner proudly waving his hundred-dollar bill to the crowd. Not recognizing the bait, an unsuspecting onlooker might then bid thirty dollars and receive only the bar of soap. Despite the mark's embarrassment and disappointment, the initial magnetism of the hundred-dollar bill fueled the bidding, which continued in a spirited manner. It went on until the crowd "began to realize that it was a put-up job to rob their pocket-books rather than replenish them, and at this juncture Smith announced that as so few cared for money, he would bid them good day." Of course, Buffam notes, "he did not go far for other dupes, and*

was soon making his generous offers to another audience."[6]

★ ★ ★ ★

Jeff Smith was born in 1860 into a well-to-do family of Georgia ministers and lawyers. It is easy to see the origins of some of the sermonlike qualities in his soap spiel: "My soap will float you over the sorrows and troubles of life and land you in the Elysian fields of perfect bliss...." Soapy's cousin, Edwin "Bobo" Smith, took the high road and became a respected newspaper editor in Washington, D.C.

What caused Soapy to take the low road? From an indifferent beginning, young Jeff took his extraordinary skills into the marketplace, and developed them alongside a certain cynicism about society that seemingly developed in the aftermath of the Civil War. The Smith family's wealth had been in land and slaves. During the war, and in the tumultuous period after it, the family lost everything. This was young Jeff's first lesson in the unfairness of life. Jeff's father, a lawyer, abandoned active practice and coped with his losses by turning to drink. In the aftermath of the war years, he moved the family west, settling in Round Rock, Texas, a small frontier settlement near modern Austin. But that was the extent of his efforts on behalf of his family.

Jeff's mother, Mabel Smith, supported herself and her family including Jeff, younger brother Bascom, and two sisters by operating a wood-frame hotel on West Baghdad Street in Round Rock. The hotel was known for the talking parrot that let forth from the front porch with an unspeakable vocabulary, reportedly acquired from Mrs. Smith, known for her hot temper.[7] A saving grace of Round Rock's economy was that it was a whistle-stop on the railroad. Young Jeff's first job was to meet the trains and persuade weary travelers to stay at his mother's establishment. Many of the railroad passengers were "delighted to learn from young Jeff that the hotel in Round Rock compared to the famed *Delmonico's*...."[8] It was his first chance to develop his own spiel, tailor it to the mark at hand and experience the thrill of its success.

His next job was working for the local general store. Here he picked up elementary marketing and public relations skills, and made himself useful enough to earn $75 a month. These small town jobs provided Jeff the beginning skills for his eventual profession. As he passed his mid-teens, Jeff looked around the community for role models to see how he could make his way in the world.

According to cousin "Bobo" Smith, Soapy's early lessons in his future profession came from an itinerant peddler, who worked on street corners, using his "fluid patter and smooth tongued voice to sell the large assortment of goods he paraded from town to town." Fascinated, young Jeff soon learned the patter of the street salesman, adding sleight of hand tricks to impress his street corner audiences. Soon he could attract a crowd and induce them to buy his cheap goods. Banking on the power of these abilities, Jeff quit his job at the general store, ordered his own stock, began peddling on his own, and succeeded in making a good return on his investment.[9]

Jeff had learned to ride early on. From time to time in their teens, Jeff and his best friend, Joe Simons, worked as drovers on cattle drives, herding local cattle first into Missouri and on the Chisholm Trail and later 650 miles north to the railroad hub in Abilene, Kansas. There he came across the circus, and the circus grifter Club-Foot Hall, an artist at the shell game. Taking up a position in the crowded midway, Hall set out his three half-walnut shells, under one of which was a dried pea. Swiftly moving the shells in circles while spieling a distracting patter, he invited his audience to bet under which shell the pea would come to rest, deftly palming the pea to increase his own odds.[10]

By all accounts, Club-Foot took on Jeff as a shill and taught him the fundamentals. A studious apprentice, Jeff soon became an artist at the shell game. He had a gift for attracting and keeping his audience, for the deft manipulation of the walnut shells, for the art of the spiel, and for the sleight of hand that ensured a fat profit. And he was beginning to grasp the psychology of enticing the sucker, which lies at the true heart of the game. David Maurer, historian and linguist of the underworld, asserts that, like Soapy, many of the later practitioners of the highly organized con games that were the forerunner to mob activities got their start in the shell game, because the alluringly simple gambit involves all the subtle aspects of the more complex escapades. "So far as psychological factors are concerned, it is the great grand-daddy of modern big confidence games."[11]

The shell game, the most elemental con game, is not an

American invention, although it has come to mean "any swindle or fraud" in American slang. It appears in eighteenth century England as the thimble-rig, a trick employing three thimbles weighted with solder. It quickly crossed to America, and became a staple of the riverboat gamblers on the Mississippi. In the mid-nineteenth century, some shell game practitioners began to attach themselves to the popular traveling circuses, and the dodge became so well known that the phrase entered the vocabulary about 1885.

Circus managers quickly recognized the shell game as a popular sideshow entertainment that drew the rubes and could be extremely lucrative. Under the protection of the circus management, the simple game developed many of the aspects of the quintessential con. Circus grifters became highly organized in league with the circus itself, which took a cut of the profits. A fixer, paid by the circus management, bribed local authorities in advance, and the day's take was divided each night in the circus privilege-car.[12]

When news came in 1877 of the new silver boom at Leadville, high in the Colorado Rockies, Jeff saw a wider field of opportunity and left the circus with which he had been traveling. Like much of the Rockies, the Leadville area had been mined for placer gold since the late 1860s. Geologist Alvinus B. Woods bought up some of the gold claims around 1875, but like all of the miners in the area, he was plagued by the black sands clogging his sluice boxes. In an unlikely mineral coup, Woods eventually identified the pesky sands as a form of silver ore, and in 1877 discovered that the sand came from a rich vein of carbonate of lead carrying an unprecedented forty ounces of silver to the ton.

Thousands of eager fortune seekers rushed to prospect for silver veins and ore bodies in the three rich gulches making up the Leadville Mining District. A former peddler from Philadelphia named Meyer Guggenheim made his first fortune on the *A.Y. Mine* and at the *Minnie* in California Gulch. In Evans Gulch, prospector and grocery owner Horace Tabor lucked into part ownership of the famous *Matchless Mine*, yielding over $100,000 a month. And way up Stray Horse Gulch, past the *Camp Bird* and the *Maid of Erin*, was the famous *Little Johnny*, source of "the unsinkable" Molly Brown's millions.[13]

The new town of Leadville was at the heart of the silver rush, one of the biggest bonanzas in Colorado history. At twelve thousand feet, far from any railroad, it was an unlikely place for permanent human habitation, and a difficult place to reach. But by the summer of 1878 it was a full-fledged boomtown with a main street lined with false-fronted saloons. Jeff Smith would have been only eighteen if he arrived that summer in Leadville. He set up his tripe and keister at the corner of Third and Harrison Streets. Already adept at sleight of hand tricks, on the wild streets of Leadville young Jeff met serious competition in the form of V. Bullock "Old Man" Taylor, legendary as the originator of the soap game, which took the street corner con to a new level.

While the shell game was old hat, the soap game was new, different, and unexpected. While the focus of the shell game was the tiny, hidden pea, in the performance of the soap game the audience could actually see the practitioner openly wrapping small bars of soap with real currency: ten-, twenty-, and even hundred-dollar bills. It seemed too good to be true.

Jeff began by working as one of Taylor's shills. When he walked up, picked out a bar of soap, and actually won a prize bill, the audience was easily enticed into the game. Jeff was a quick learner, and it was not long before he mastered the game, and his operation surpassed Taylor's own.

By 1879, the newly wealthy H. A. W. Tabor had built himself and his new town a wonderful opera house that was soon to host the iconoclastic British writer and performance artist Oscar Wilde. Across the alley, entrepreneur Bill Bush built a three-storey hotel he called the Clarion. Leadville was soon too civilized for Taylor and Soapy both; everyone there had already been fleeced once, and there were no more strangers. They parted ways, apparently amicably, with Taylor heading east, while his protégé Jefferson Randolph Smith, still not twenty-one, resolved to seek his fortune in Denver.

Thanks to the new silver discoveries Denver, the metropolis between the plains and the Rockies, was booming, growing from a provincial population of 4,759 in 1870 to 35,629 by 1880. Thousands of midwestern farmhands and naïve easterners seeking their fortunes disembarked the main train lines before boarding smaller lines or stagecoaches in order to reach the mining camps in the mountains. Lower downtown Denver, the area now popularly called LoDo, was a boomtown within a growing city, close to the train station and positioned to attract the crowds before they were siphoned off to downtown. Larimer and Market Streets were lined with dance halls, gambling establishments, and saloons, which ran wide-open, twenty-four hours a day. Madams including Mattie Silks clustered their bordellos on Holladay Street and did a lively trade. All these enterprises operated in spite of laws ostensibly outlawing both gambling and prostitution. But small fines served only as de facto license fees that the police were happy to collect in exchange for looking the other way. With the police used to tolerating the criminal element, Denver was a town that was tailor-made for organized gangs, a situation which Jeff Smith would soon learn to exploit.

Denver's most famous establishment, the *Arcade* on Larimer Street, opened as a high priced restaurant in 1880, next door to the infamous *Murphy's Exchange*. Mining men, stock speculators, and business men made it a central watering hole while Denver's growing fraternity of newspaper men regularly dropped in for midnight suppers. Up the street stood the new *Windsor Hotel*, and across the street rose the brand new and extravagant Tabor Block, all the result of the silver wealth flowing out of Leadville. But in the spirit of a frontier boomtown, the area was plagued with violent brawls, muggings, bar fights, shootings, and not a few murders.

The shooting of Jim Moon is still remembered as one of the most notorious killings. In early 1881 Jim Moon, a kind of town bully, opened a gambling hall on the second floor of the *Arcade*. His short tenure as an entrepreneur ended on June 16, 1881 when another sporting man, Clay Wilson, approached Moon on the floor of the gaming hall, then shot and killed him in cold blood, apparently to avenge Moon's numerous predations. Big Ed Chase, already a power in gambling circles, took over the operation, while Wilson was ever after known as the killer of Jim Moon.

The young Jeff Smith was nineteen when he first visited Denver in 1879.[14] He made a number of return trips, finally making Denver his headquarters. Still a neophyte at the art of fleecing suckers, he devoted himself to establishing his reputation in the hierarchy of the Denver underworld. While perfecting the delivery of his soap spiel in these early years, he may have resorted to petty crime. Meanwhile, to hide his real age, Soapy grew the Civil War-style black beard, and adopted the broad brimmed black hat that would become his trademark for the next twenty years. By June 1880, he had already been arrested for displaying a pistol. He was fined in police court at the end of 1881, and then charged with larceny as bailee in March of 1882.[15] On one of these occasions, the charge was selling soap without a license. The arresting officer, already quite familiar with Jeff Smith's frequent and very public street corner performance, neglected his real name, and simply listed him in the police register as "Soapy," thus conferring the famous moniker.

Soapy usually held forth on busy 17th Street, just a few blocks from the Union train station with its formidable clock tower and flanking horse cab stables. He pulled up in a wagon, set up his tripe and keister and made a visibly elaborate ceremony out of wrapping his bars of soap in blue paper, and arranging them in the case. Then he began his patter, the heart of the soap scheme:

> *Gentlemen, the all-important question which I propound to you and for which I earnestly seek the answer is this: How are you fixed for soap?*
>
> *But seriously, though my message is that of soap, it is likewise a message of hope. For today to meet that need which is so apparent in you, I bring a new soap a wonder soap. Here is the finest cleansing product ever brought forth by man's scientific ingenuity, the fruit of many weary months of patient research and experiment in my own laboratories. Use this soap upon your skin, and it will shine like the moon, and your face will gleam with the radiance of the sun at noonday....*[16]

Carstenphen, in his letter to the editor, remembered that after the show, he saw Soapy enter the *Arcade*, and walk proudly through a crowd of admirers, the center of attention. "All who had seen his performance during the day anxiously waited to see how he would do at the faro tables. Soapy didn't use chips. Instead he emptied his pockets of a large stack of twenty-dollar gold pieces, and wagered them as fast as his bets could be taken. At first he won, but afterwards he lost heavily, until it was rumored that he was dead broke. Then, he would appeal to Big Ed Chase who gladly staked him to another roll to win it all back at the soap game the next day."[17]

While Soapy was barely out of his teens when he arrived in 1879, Ed Chase was a tall mature man of forty and had been a fixture of the clubs since opening the *Progressive Gambling Parlor* in 1872. If anyone could be said to be in control of the saloon and gambling district in these years it was Chase. For Soapy, like many others, faro was an addiction. He spent many evenings in the *Arcade* after Ed Chase took it over, betting on faro with all the money he made from the miners and cowboys on the street. Denver folklore has it that "he lost more money at faro than any other man in the history of Denver, and old-time gamblers do not dispute the claim."[18]

"At the close of the performance with Chase's money in his pocket, Soapy walked out of the hall as nonchalantly as he had entered." And the next day, there he was again at 17th Street with the tripe and keister.[19]

Denver's active gambling scene attracted all of the West's major gambling figures, including William Barclay "Bat" Masterson, and his sidekick, professional gambler Wyatt Earp. Large gaming halls, like today's Las Vegas casinos, provided employment to professional gamblers like Earp, and Masterson, who eventually owned the Palace himself. The gambling halls needed these professional players to provide the backbone of expertise and trustworthiness for these essentially honest games. In private club rooms, expert players like Masterson and Earp matched wits at high-stakes poker games with newly minted millionaires such as Horace Tabor.

Denver was just one stop along a gambler's circuit of wide-open western towns where the quasi-legal gambling industry was tolerated, if not embraced. According to Western historian Robert K. DeArment, "It was an article of faith on the frontier that the degree of prosperity of a town was in direct proportion to the number of high rolling gamblers on hand at a given time."[20]

Soapy's days on the street and nights at the faro tables might have gone on indefinitely, if he had not varied his routine by venturing into the nearby *Palace Theater.* It was said that Ed Chase got into the theater business after the owner of a theater troupe lost his payroll at one of the faro tables at his *Progressive Gambling Parlor.* Deciding to make the most of his new gains, Chase and his partner Hub Heatly built the large and commodious brick building on

Blake Street to house their new theater troupe. Downstairs, the *Palace* boasted Denver's largest and most elaborate gambling hall, accommodated two hundred players and twenty-five dealers.

Upstairs the 750-seat theater featured variety and vaudeville acts of all sorts, but it was the female performers who drew the crowd. "The bill usually opens with songs of the day sung by a bevy of young women seated in crescent formation.... One by one the girls step to the footlights and offer their song selections interspersed with jokes from the comedians. Many of the young women are known as serio-comic songsters and early in the act each is dressed in skirts falling to about the knees."[21] Henry Martyn Hart, dean of St. John's Cathedral, condemned the theater, calling it "a death trap to young men, a foul den of vice and corruption,"[22] thus indirectly testifying to its popularity.

The winsome attractiveness of these young women was illustrated by Ed Chase himself who was the first of the *Palace* owners to marry one of the songbirds. After years of infamous and well-publicized womanizing, including two other marriages, Chase married Frances Minerva, one of the celebrated Barbour Sisters in 1880. Next, Chase's partner Ed Gaylord married the other Barbour sister, Addie. Perhaps following their example, Bat Masterson married Palace song and dance girl Emma Walters in 1882.

Soapy's epiphany came one night after watching yet another Palace cabaret performance of one of his favorites, golden-voiced Anna Neilson, a singer and actress known as "Allie." Soapy had been watching the charming young woman tread the boards night after night, and noticed that she never fraternized with the patrons, but kept modestly to herself. As he waited behind the stage for her one night he saw another man accost her roughly. Soapy attacked the other man, then escorted the lovely singer home, and pressed his suit over the following days. They were married in February 1886.[23]

It was a new era for Soapy. In another instance of Soapy's split personality, he installed his new bride in a modern bungalow in a nice neighborhood of Denver, far from the gambling and prostitution of Larimer Street. For many years after, few of his associates even knew he was married. Yet he and Anna apparently had a happy home life as well as five children over the years. But it was an attack on Anna's reputation that led to one of Soapy's most famous brawls.

Confidence Men and Bunco Steerers

It's just as easy to make big money as little money. In my profession, a hundred dollars is just chicken feed. We think in thousands, not tens. Experience has taught me that it is as easy to separate a sucker, the right sucker, from five thousand dollars as from fifty.

We always offered our services to well-to-do men, holding out the promise that their investments were certain to net them profit in three or four figures, at least and that's the real bait for the sucker, particularly if he's the close-fisted kind that always wants something for nothing. Yes, there always was a lot of satisfaction as well as cash profit in trimming some old skin flint who would rob his grandmother if he had a chance.

Doc Baggs[24]

While Soapy was finding his legs in Denver as a petty criminal, two-bit thimble rigger, and inveterate gambler at the faro tables, the real action in the up and coming crime capital in the Rockies was the growing sophistication and organization in the world of pure bunco: the confidence games that are as old as time, and as fresh as the latest sucker. "Doc" Charles Baggs was their chief professional practitioner in Denver, and his game reached its apex after the opening of the new *Union Pacific Station* in 1881.

Baggs practiced his art on the streets of Denver using one of many disguises from his trunk full of costumes: a stockman, ranchman, banker, or his most famous, a minister with a Bible under his right arm. Like most con men, Baggs followed the big money, and it is no surprise he was in Leadville during its boom years, where undoubtedly he and Soapy became well acquainted. As in all trades, the young men learn by apprenticing themselves to the masters, and Baggs was a master at his trade.

Soapy was one of the great con artists of his time, "the Monarch of Misrule." However, ultimately it is clear that everything that Soapy put into play in Skagway he had learned earlier working with Baggs and others in Denver. A young prospector from Astoria,

Mont Hawthorne, who had seen Soapy in the flesh, described him in his Alaskan heyday as "a nice-mannered clean-looking fellow. He never went around talking and bragging and shoving folks. He moved quiet and soft-like, but he was always figgering out how things was best for Soapy every minute."[25]

Soapy himself was not unique. In fact, he was perhaps the archetypal con man. In regards to the confidence men themselves, historian David Maurer describes the type: "Confidence men are not 'crooks' in the ordinary sense of the word. They are suave, slick and capable." Further, he notes that they typically are highly intelligent and able to put together a solid organization.[26]

One of the origins of bunco was on the great Mississippi riverboats, where cardsharps and shell game artists preyed upon the wealthy passengers who were willing to gamble. Maurer, the only scholar to have thoroughly studied the con man's art, emphasizes that the simple shell game is in fact primarily a game of psychology and embodies all of the elements of the more elaborate cons. "While most spectators assume that the basis of the shell game is sleight of hand, and that the victim is taken in by the manual skill of the player, and while this belief is encouraged by most operators who can be counted on to call attention to that old saw that says that the hand is faster than the eye, in truth, the grifters depend more upon the psychology of the confidence game than upon spectacular skill."[27] From the riverboats and the river towns, the games and their practitioners gravitated to the itinerant world of the traveling circuses. Working the large free-spending crowds attracted by the holiday atmosphere and excitement of the circus, the skilled shell game artist employed both steerers and shills who made fake bets, and were paid off with fake winnings, all in a carefully scripted and choreographed play. The grifters developed a tight organization, which was the forerunner of the organization of the con gang itself. Once Jeff Smith became attuned to the psychology of the shell game and of the sucker, he was well positioned to take up the challenges of the big con.

From the riverboats, circus lots, and racetracks, the action moved to the notorious camps that followed the construction of the *Union Pacific Railroad*. The temporary shanty towns collectively known as "Hell on Wheels" grew with ever increasing numbers of gamblers, prostitutes, saloons, and dance halls, and the thimble riggers and sure-thing men who accompanied them. The whole tent city was packed up and traveled behind the train on flat cars, to be rebuilt at each camp.

By the time the rolling red-light district reached Cheyenne in 1867-68, nearly every well-known gambler in the West had made an appearance. Grifter Ben Marks, Doc Baggs, Canada Bill Jones, Frank Tarbeaux, John Bull and riverboat gambler George Devol were all there. Trading tricks and techniques, the assembled con men gave birth to the basic structure of the modern con game. In a major innovation in the games, Ben Marks, who made his way west dealing three-card monte, came up with the idea for the "Dollar Store." Finding the competition tough for his street corner setup, he opened a fake store and stocked the front window with expensive merchandise all marked "one dollar." The whole store was contrived and set up especially to lure the unsuspecting, bargain hunting mark into a protected environment where he could be suckered into a crooked game and fleeced. The dollar store was the forerunner of the "Big Store," one of the central features of all the later big-time confidence games.[28]

From hell-on-wheels towns like Cheyenne and Laramie, the core practitioners spread out across the country developing variations of the basic scripts simultaneously in many different places over the next twenty years. The principals, such as Ben Marks in Omaha and Council Bluffs, and Doc Baggs in Denver, took on the role of fixers, needed to maintain quasi-legal appearances and accepted social relationships in a certain locale. They might leave a sizeable donation in the church collection plate one day, and be cheating at cards in the local saloon the next.

These operators trained and relied on a bevy of steerers, cappers, sticks, and shills, a population that was unusually itinerant, so there was soon a large and highly organized floating population of skilled con men. Moving from one place to another, sharing innovations, skilled confidence men soon standardized many aspects of the games. The renewed and improved bunco games became a fixture of Mississippi River steamboats, cross-country trains, and big and small cities across the country.[29] The con man's art form thrived on, and became an ironic underground parallel of the get-rich-quick mentality that drove the West, and later became a mainstay of the mobs of the twentieth century.

The scams practiced and polished first in Denver and Creede and later operated to the hilt in Skagway adhered to the very specific principles and mob organization that all con games, big and small, follow. Invariably the organized gang includes a specific cast of actors, each with an assigned role to play. The outside man, roper, or steerer, works the street and ropes the mark into the game. The inside man is the main player who works the shell game in the simplest version, or the stock swindle in a more complex version. The fixer, often the most powerful man in the gang, controlled all of the payoffs to police and politicians. The gang also employed various shills, or sticks, the bit players in the carefully scripted street dramas.[30]

Following careful interviews in the course of his research in Chicago in the 1930s, Maurer distilled certain principles underlying all confidence games, big and little, and includes the gang argot:

1. *Locating and investigating the well-to-do victim (Putting up the mark).*
2. *Gaining the victim's confidence (playing the con for him).*
3. *Steering him to meet the inside man (roping the mark).*
4. *Permitting the inside man to show him how he can make a large amount of money dishonestly (telling him the tale).*
5. *Allowing the victim to make a substantial profit (giving him the convincer).*
6. *Determining exactly how much he will invest (giving him the breakdown).*
7. *Playing him against a big store and fleecing him (taking off the touch).*
8. *Getting him out of the way as quietly as possible (blowing him off).*
9. *Forestalling action by the law (putting in the fix).*[31]

Jeff Smith grew up in the exciting world of the Denver underground and matured along with the maturing of the con game itself, working with veteran Doc Baggs as he transformed himself from a two-bit thimble rigger to a skilled, and sometimes ruthless, fixer.

Doc Baggs had operated in Denver from the early 1870s and assembled a retinue of cappers. He seldom made use of cards, preferring to play for higher stakes. He usually was cunning enough to avoid prosecution. Baggs opened his first Big Store in Denver 1881, when the new *Union Station* was completed. This coincided with the decline of Leadville as a raw boomtown, and the movement of most of the action to Denver, following the money. Baggs had the smarts and the money to finance the big scams, and the reputation among the promising members of the underworld. Soapy, though enterprising and a fast talker, was still under twenty-one. This began a four-year heyday for Soapy. While he was learning about the Big Con, the organization, and the plays from Baggs, he was running his own soap game on his favorite corner, using his own ropers and shills, and gambling all night at the *Arcade*.

The Doctor's *Big Store* was a well-appointed, second-floor suite just up the street from the new train station, similar in every respect to those occupied by successful real estate and stock brokers. The well-dressed office staff sat on high stools, entering transactions into large, leatherbound ledger books, or hurried about their business from one private office to another. On the far side of the main office, behind the solid oak counter, with railing and gate, an immense safe was built into the wall, its massive door open to reveal the customary shelves and pigeonholes. Bagg's large and imposing desk stood directly in front of the safe.[32]

The key to the whole game was that the sucker had to agree in advance to participate in a scheme that was illegal: a fixed bet, an inside stock tip, a fixed footrace or horse race. Doc Baggs used a number of ropers or steerers who appeared to be ordinary business-men, to finger likely marks on the streets of Denver, usually at the train station, and set them up for the con. The steerer would nonchalantly start up a conversation with a visiting businessman who looked to be well heeled. Once in the office, the sucker would be led through a confusing series of stock trades, or bets, in which he seemed at first to win an enormous sum, setting him up for the big sting. Now anxious to make a killing himself, the over-anxious mark would invariably pull out his bankroll and actually hand it over to Baggs, never to see it again.

Sometimes, the mark would be lured into the offices only to

be suckered into a phony poker game with a whole table of shills, where he inevitably lost his money. At other times, a fake bust would be staged with phony policemen, during which the sucker would be robbed.[33]

In the aftermath of all these plays, the gang counted on the sucker not to complain to the police. What businessman wanted to let it be known that he had been suckered by a bunco gang? If the victim did decide to go to the police, he would find them unsympathetic, or perhaps appearing to look for the perpetrators, but ultimately confused. Of course, Baggs and his gang had taken pains to pay off the cops; the fix was another major element of the bunco game.

If the stranger endeavored to look for the offices of the crooks, he might lead the cop to the site, only to find that it had vanished. In fact, the whole office was a stage set: oak counters, folding partitions, papier-mâché ledger books and all. The immense safe itself was just a trompe L'oeil work of art with an inspired perspective view into its interior. It was painted realistically on a number of thin wooden panels joined together with silk. Doc Baggs could quickly remove it from the wall and walk out with it under his arm.

Baggs ultimately trained an entire new generation of bunco artists including the young Soapy Smith during the course of the early 1880s. Every one of the office workers was a shill. Together with the ropers and steerers who worked the street, they made up the growing gang, recruited from the ranks of gamblers and grifters hanging around Denver. Baggs' fake offices were a prime example of the *Big Store*, a stage set on which were enacted scenes from a classic con rip-off. Soapy later copied many of these same elements in his fake storefronts in Skagway.

Many of the other actors in Baggs' games had also been in on the action in Cheyenne, including Clay Wilson, Baggs' future partner, and Jim Moon. Others who participated included Tom Cady, a three-card-monte man; Gene Laughlin, wizard of the fixed roulette wheel; cardsharp Cliff Sparks; Tom Daniels, leading capper; George Millsap, crooked faro dealer; and Cal Somers, George Wilder, the "Reverend" Bowers, J. B. Parmer, Billy Kelly, Con Sullivan, and John Bull.[34]

Soapy Smith was a quick learner, and while participating in

Doc Baggs' game, he also began to orchestrate con jobs of his own, and was already beginning to exhibit his talents as a fixer.

By 1884, *Rocky Mountain News* editor Colonel John Arkins was fed up with the lawlessness in downtown Denver. He ran a vendetta in the pages of his paper against the bunco men, announcing his intentions with the headline: "Bunco deals robbing the miners." Then, in the pages of his paper he publicly challenged Sheriff Michael Spangler to do something about it. Sheriff Spangler stepped in over the compromised authority of the local chief of police and announced that Baggs and his confidence men must go. Baggs was charged with being a bunco steerer, and spent part of a day in jail. But the wily Baggs, acting as his own attorney, argued that the term "bunco-steerer" appeared nowhere in the legal statutes, and was not even in the dictionary, and therefore, was not prohibited. Apparently, the argument convinced Judge Victor Elliott, who let Baggs walk out of the courtroom.[35]

But Spangler was not through with Baggs. He detailed Deputy Emil Auspitz to tail Baggs everywhere he went and to head off or warn potential victims. Baggs at first thought this was a huge joke, and used his entire supply of costumes and disguises in an elaborate cat and mouse game with the deputy. But in the end, Spangler's strategy had the desired effect and Baggs left Denver. City detective Mart Watrous remembered the event. When he boarded a train to take a prisoner to a southern city, he recognized many of Baggs' associates, but not Baggs himself, who was justly smug about his disguise.[36]

Baggs today is unheard of, his career little known, perhaps because he was never successfully prosecuted even though the Pinkerton detectives were well aware of his swindles. Few of the suckers he skinned pursued the law for redress, and if they did, Baggs had a solution. He always had one of his henchmen trail the victim, and if he headed for the police, Baggs' man intervened, and arranged a meeting, where Baggs offered to give back part of the money, to avoid a scandal.

Baggs was about forty in 1885 when he was forced out of Denver. As Baggs' career illustrates, the key to con success was to remain unknown, operating always under the radar of the police. Baggs seems to have avoided the hot-headed syndrome that doomed

Soapy and many another con men. Many if not most con men succumb to the desire to be recognized for their abilities and end up as alcoholics with a flamboyant lifestyle. After all, what use is it to have robbed someone of thousands of dollars when no one knows?

Baggs avoided the braggart syndrome, and successfully maintained a low profile most of the time. On the road again after leaving Denver, he took up the gold brick scheme and other scams with his new associate, Clay Wilson, always remembered in Denver as the killer of Jim Moon. Baggs' experience in Colorado enabled him to talk volubly and convincingly of veins, ore-occurrence, stopes, sumps, dips, angles, spurs, and sidelines. This mastery of mining jargon helped him to interest suckers in phantom riches in the form of a gold brick. The gold brick scheme involved selling a faux gold brick with an elaborate story about a lost Mexican mine, or the booty from an old stagecoach robbery. In 1891 Baggs and Wilson swindled an Eastern man out of $30,000, and two mining men out of another $15,000.

Baggs disappeared entirely until 1912, when his partner Wilson was arrested in Dayton, Ohio, after the pair pulled one more con. Wilson was sentenced to three years, but appealed, then jumped bond and disappeared. By 1915, Baggs had passed the ripe old age of 70, but he surfaced in San Diego, still pulling the occasional successful swindle.[37]

Doc Baggs' exit from Denver in 1885 did not end the city's bunco operations. Instead, it left an opening that was tailor-made for the twenty-five-year-old Soapy Smith. Soapy adopted Baggs' techniques wholesale, and assumed leadership of the gang that Baggs had assembled. By 1889, just four years later, Soapy was clearly in charge. Many of the members of this gang from the late 1880s would stick with Soapy, and ultimately follow him to Skagway.

The "Reverend" Charles Bowers, Soapy's right-hand man in Skagway, had been a part of the organization since Soapy's early days in Denver. Of an older generation than Soapy, Bowers was already an employee at the *Palace Theater* in January 1879, before Soapy arrived.[38] In those early days, there is some evidence that Bowers was involved in petty thievery.[39] But by the 1890s his methods had subtly evolved and he had become an important member of the bunco organization. The Rev. Bowers was one of those involved in a fight at Soapy Smith's short-lived Denver saloon, the *Tivoli*, in 1892.[40]

A smooth talker, and one of the more intellectual members of the group, Bowers became one of the chief steerers of the organization. His specialty was as a "glad-hander" or "grip man." Frequenting the hotels and the train station, he would look for the pins or emblems of the secret societies and fraternal orders of the day: the *Elks*, *Eagles*, *Odd-Fellows*, *Masons*, *Knights of Pythias*, and so forth. Having memorized the appropriate secret greeting and handshakes for each, he could greet any member as a brother, and in a short time, steer him to one of Soapy's elaborate cons or card games, while gathering enough information to dupe him.

"Judge" van Horn, another gang member, had in fact begun his career in the legal profession and perhaps served as a justice of the peace. He became well known as a jury fixer, and for taking advantage of quirks in the law, in which capacity he was to prove useful to Soapy.

Van Tripplett, known as "Old Man Trip," also became one of Soapy's chief followers, and one of the first to follow him to Skagway. His white beard and lined visage perfectly suited the role of experienced prospector, which allowed him to gain the confidence of those he met on the trail whether in Colorado or Alaska. Syd Dixon was another shining star in the universe of the gang, capable of working elaborate confidence games. The son of a wealthy family, Dixon was a disbarred attorney and playboy of some renown. After traveling the world, he had become hooked on opium, and, having squandered his fortune, was estranged from his family. Yet, with his dress, bearing, and mannerisms he could still convincingly play the part of a wealthy easterner.

W. H. Jackson had quietly acted as a part of Soapy's elite bunco gang at least since 1889. Jackson's skills at creating "false-fronts" would be well used in the new enterprises in Skagway. Red Gibbs was one of the group's heavies, ready to spring into physical action should there be trouble. Other names on the gang's roster included "Eat-'em up" Jake Cohen; Dolly Brooks, the Duke of Halstead Street; ladies' man Jimmy Thornton; Big Ed Burns; Tom Daniels; Cliff Sparks; George Millsap; Frisco Red Harris; J. B. Parmer; Billy Kelly; Con Sullivan; Ice Box Murphy; and Jimmy Bruce, "The

Great Gobblefish." Banjo Parker and Fatty Gray were also among the gang's heavies, enforcers who were not shy about using force.[41] "Slim Jim" Foster was just a youngster when he joined the gang in its last years in Denver. He was only twenty-two in the fall of 1897 when he joined Soapy in Skagway at the first summons.[42]

There is no night in Creede

Here's a land where all are equal
of high or lowly birth.
A land where men make millions
Dug from the dreary earth.
Here the meek and mild-eyed burros
on mineral mountains feed.
It's day all day in the daytime,
and there is no night in Creede.

The cliffs are solid silver
with wondrous wealth untold,
And the beds of running rivers
are lined with glittering gold.
While the world is filled with sorrow
and hearts must break and bleed,
It's day all day in the daytime,
and there is no night in Creede.
Cy Warman, *"the poet of the Rockies"*
The Trail, January 1920, pp 12-13.

When the great excitement came
Everyone that played the game
Square or sure that could succeed,
Packed his grip and came to Creede.
Miners, merchants, maques, and marks,
Surething men and bunco sharks,
Men of money, men of greed,
Everyone fetched up at Creede.
Billy DeVere, from "Jeff and Joe"

The new town of Creede was booming in the summer of 1891, deep in an impossibly narrow gulch carved by Willow Creek in the San Juan Mountains of southwest Colorado. Like most boomtowns in Colorado and elsewhere, it seemed to spring to life overnight. After the discovery of silver by Nicholas Creede, railroad tycoon Dave Moffat laid the foundations of a real boom. He purchased an interest in Nicholas Creede's claims, and ran a spur of his *Denver and Rio Grande Railroad* the remaining ten miles from Wagon Wheel Gap. When the railroad reached the new town in December 1890, Denver silver and gold seekers from the East could reach Creede directly, without spending a single dusty day on the trail. The *Denver and Rio Grande Railroad* carried hundreds of adventurers to the small valley, and freighted tons of ore out. It paid for its cost of construction in four months.[43]

Like most boomtowns, Creede began as a row of tents along a muddy main street. Richard Harding Davis described it in *Harper's Monthly*:

> *Not a brick, a painted front nor an awning in the whole town. It is like a city of fresh cardboard. In the street are ox teams, mules, men, and donkeys loaded with ore crowding each other familiarly and sinking knee deep in mud. Furniture and kegs, cases and piles of raw lumber heaped up in front of the new stores ... it is more like a circus tent which has sprung up and may be removed on the morrow than a town.*[44]

Back in Denver, Soapy was losing his precious anonymity. Soapy and the gang had begun boldly harassing the Denver citizens at Logan Park, where Denverites picnicked. In harassing the ordinary residents of Denver, Soapy's gang had clearly stepped over the line. As purported gang leader, Soapy had made deals with the police to fleece only strangers, but this would be one of the first instances where he lost control of the actions of his gang members. The predations of the mob degenerated into a general free-for-all, and the police had to react.

While Soapy and the gang attempted to make themselves scarce until things quieted down, the *Rocky Mountain News* continued its campaign against the hoodlums and their puppet master, drawing unwanted attention to their activities in an article titled "Soapy's Quiet Sneak":

> *Soapy, in the language of the fly-by-night fraternity "has" Denver... He has it to do with what he will in so far as all professional swindling*

> *and stealing is concerned.... The city is absolutely under the control of this prince of knaves, and there is not a confidence man, a sneak thief, or any other parasite upon the public who does not pursue his avocation under license from the man who has become great through the power vested in him by those whose sworn duty it is to administer the laws out of fear or favor.*[45]

The *News* alleged that Soapy had sent out his men in small groups to fleece Palmer Lake, South Park, Boulder, and Georgetown, and then continued to report that in fact business was bad.

> *He will not mind a little thing like that though, his enterprises are upon too sure a footing to be bothered about a slight reverse. His skin games in town are flourishing, he gets his percentage from those to whom he furnishes protection just the same as usual. His revenue will not be materially decreased. It would be wise for the small towns to prepare a few clubs for Soapy. The Sunday picnic trade around Denver is getting desperately dull and he is an enterprising gentleman who will reach out after all that is going.*

These accusations by *News* editor Arkins were an irritant, but all part of the business. However, in Soapy's mind, Arkins stepped over the line when he included in one article a reference to Soapy's wife, then summering with Denver's society matrons at Idaho Springs. Anna's reputation as the wife of a Denver businessman was ruined, and Soapy was incensed and set his mind on immediate retaliation.

Accompanied by Banjo Parker, one of his heavies, Smith stalked Arkins, waiting for him in front of the newspaper's offices on July 30, 1889. When the editor appeared, Soapy savagely beat him with his walking stick. Soapy was of course apprehended, as there were numerous witnesses to the attack. At a preliminary hearing, the prosecution wanted to charge Smith with attempted murder, but in the end the charge was reduced to assault. Freed on $1000 bond, he somehow never came to trial.

Following Soapy's assault on Arkins, Soapy's wife Anna Smith took the children and moved back to St. Louis. Soapy, hoping his notoriety would blow over, quit Denver for a time, taking some of his gang with him, including Bowers, "Troublesome Tom" Cady,

Fatty Gray, and Tom Crippen. They worked the smaller towns in the area: Cheyenne, Wyoming; Salt Lake City and Odgen, Utah; and Pocatello, Idaho.

Although Soapy managed to survive the first fracas with Arkins, the editor turned up the heat on the gang through the summer of 1889 with a continuing series of articles: "*Soapy in the Soup: Extensive Review of his Activities*" (August 6); "*Why are bunco and confidence men allowed to remain in Denver?*" (August 11); "*Soapy Smith, his methods of operation, how his organization was built up*" and "*Thugs and thieves... Soapy's followers*" (August 18). Those articles were followed by "*Soapy did not know he was doing wrong*" (August 21); "*Gamblers held up Soapy on war path*" (August 28); and finally, "*A gang of outlaws driven out of Denver*" (September 1).[46]

In Pocatello, Soapy again ran into trouble, the fallout from previous action in Denver. Kid Kelly, the "Rincon Kid," had moved into the Idaho railroad company town, and taken control after Smith had banished him from Denver earlier in the year. When Smith and his associates tried to move in, Kelly gave them orders to quit the town in no uncertain terms. In the ensuing gunfight, one man was hit in the leg, leading to Soapy's arrest. Pocatello officials got rid of both gangs, sending them off on trains in opposite directions. Soapy and his gang moved back to Ogden, and then on to Spokane Falls, Washington, another town benefiting from the gold rush to the Coeur d'Alene district.

Soapy was only too glad to return to Denver in the spring of 1891 after the latest efforts at reform had played themselves out. He quickly opened the *Tivoli Saloon and Gambling Hall* at the corner of 17th and Market Streets. It was at the Tivoli that Soapy was inspired to post the Latin caution Caveat Emptor -"*Let the Buyer Beware*,"- at the entrance to the gambling parlor. To Soapy, this was fair enough warning for any who entered that the odds were against him. He declared in typical two-faced fashion:

> *My gambling hall is an institution of public education. Those afflicted with the gambling urge can be permanently cured, for they have no chance of winning.*

When two men complained to the police after losing $1500 at the *Tivoli*, Soapy was arrested and appeared before the Fire and

Police Commission. His extemporaneous speech in front of the court became an instant classic:

> *As a matter of fact, gentlemen, I wish to assure you that we should not be classed as gamblers. We do not conduct a gambling establishment. We are reformers in the true sense of the word! There are many so-called legitimate gambling places run openly in this city where the victims play day after day and night after night. I conduct no such unsavory business. At the* Tivoli *I am running an educational institution. The famous* Keely Institute *provides a cure for the drinking habit. At the Tivoli I have a cure for the gambling habit. The man who steps into my place is faced with the sign, "Caveat Emptor," which hangs upon the wall. That is the danger beacon, a warning to all to slow up before rounding the curve. The stranger is not compelled to play, he must use his own judgment. But if he wants to play, he is not discouraged. Why should we tell him it is useless to buck our tables? Let him learn for himself from actual experience. So we take him in hand and give him a cure for the gambling habit. He has, of course no chance of winning a cent because, in my games, the player cannot win. When he leaves he has learned a valuable lesson, one which he will never forget. He is disappointed, naturally, but he has had experience of the greatest value. In fact, gentlemen, I should be recognized as a public benefactor!*[47]

The plaster was hardly dry at Soapy's *Tivoli* when news of a new silver boom at Creede hit Denver. Having attempted to leave Denver and been discouraged or rebuffed at numerous other western towns, Soapy was eternally on the lookout for the perfect town. He remembered fondly the early days in Leadville, when every stranger seemed to be a sucker, everyone who got off the train was looking for a gold mine and easy money, and the town government was too unorganized to even recognize a gang, let alone fight back.

In the back of his mind was the formula for the perfect site. First, it would be a very small town with no town government, so that he could install his friends and associates in office. If he controlled the government himself there would be fewer officials or cops to pay off, reducing his overhead costs. Second, it must be a very new town: men with money to invest flocked to such towns. Creede fit the bill perfectly.

By this time, Soapy had in place a well-organized gang and Creede was his first opportunity to try out his new system. With silver flowing down from rich mines on the mountainsides, and men and women flowing in from Denver trying to get a piece of the action, Creede was an ideal laboratory for greed and avarice, just the right size for Soapy to develop his potent mix of con game and town management.

When news of the rich silver strike in the San Juan Mountains reached a peak, Soapy left the *Tivoli* in the hands of several trusted lieutenants and made his move. He arrived in Creede to find that Bob Ford had already opened *Ford's Exchange* and was taking a percentage from the prostitutes upstairs as well as the shell games in the streets. According to many, Ford was attempting to proclaim himself boss of Creede. Known nearly everywhere as the cowardly murderer of Jesse James, Ford was another man who needed the anonymity of the frontier.

Also residing in Creede at this time was square gambler and gun man Bat Masterson, managing the Denver Exchange for former detective Mart Watrous, now a Denver gambling entrepreneur. Bat was as honest a gambler as the definition allowed. Widely respected for his calm, cool, and even-handed judgment, he had been hired to keep order at the gambling hall, a necessity in the face of yet another boomtown where there was literally no law and order on the streets, and he performed his job effectively. Masterson and Soapy Smith were well acquainted from Denver. Though Soapy was on the crooked side, and Bat was a straight shooter, they were friends, and had a grudging respect for each other.

The town was quiet for the first few months, which worried Masterson. As he remarked to one of his dealers:

> *I don't like this quiet, it augers ill. I have been in several places that started out this way and there were generally wild scenes of carnage before many weeks passed... It seems as if there must be a little blood-letting to get things into proper working order.*[48]

Creede was indeed perfect for Soapy's experiment. There was no government at all until February 1892, when Soapy took control and got a handpicked slate of "businessmen" elected to a town council, while his brother-in-law was appointed Chief of Police.

With this minimal organization and his protection racket, Soapy maintained nominal control over the town and provided a modicum of protection from escalating violence for the ordinary citizens, but he was either not able or not interested in preventing a series of murders, as predicted by Masterson.

Meanwhile, Soapy opened his own *Orleans Club*, and was joined there by his boyhood friend from the *Chisholm Trail*, Joe Simons. Until the *Orleans Club* got out of the red, they apparently slept on the gambling tables. Although the club eventually paid off, this happy state of affairs was not destined to last more than a few months. Simons took ill with pneumonia, and no amount of Soapy's money or medical attention was able to save him. When Simons finally succumbed on March 19, 1892, Soapy was deeply demoralized. Simon's sad death and his gambler's burial were immortalized in Colorado mountain verse by "tramp poet" Billy DeVere, in "Jeff and Joe." In the poem we perhaps find the origins of Soapy's reputation as a genuine frontier good guy. DeVere lauds him for staying true to his friend, and arranging the burial just as Joe wanted it.

They drank and sang; the pure white snow
Fell softly on the grave of Joe.
And as for Jeff, well I can say,
No better man exists today.
I don't mean good the way you do,
No not religious, only true;
True to himself, true to his friend.

Don't quit nor weaken to the end;
And I can say, if any can,
That Jeff will help his fellow man;
And here I thank him don't you see,
For kindness he has shown to me.

[The entire poem appears at the close of this chapter.]

Depressed and despondent, nearly undone by the death of his good friend, Soapy nevertheless pulled himself together a few weeks later as he smelled more money to be made. His emotional rebirth was triggered by the arrival of a talisman of great good fortune, a concrete sculpture in the shape of a huge man.

Bob Fitzsimmons, a gambler, had gone to Denver and invested in the cement likeness of an oversized human figure. He carefully transported it to Creede under the cover of night and buried it in the hills, where his associate, J. J. Dore, conveniently "discovered it" a few days later, on April 9, 1892. Fitzsimmons placed the "petrified man" on display in the *Hotel Vaughn*, charged twenty-five cents a person, to view the perfectly preserved remains, and created an instant sensation.

Not wanting to miss out on a swindle, Soapy and some of his associates stole the petrified giant, moved him to the back room of the *Orleans Club* and displayed him under the dim, eerie light of kerosene lamps shaded with intentionally blackened chimneys. They named the relic "Colonel Stone."

While Soapy perfected his new understanding of the infant science of anthropology and shaped it into a spiel that he itched to deliver to the crowds, Fitzsimmons sued to recover his property. Eventually the two sharpsters reached a congenial agreement to split the profits.

> *"See Col. Stone!" went the spiel. "He roamed these hills, a giant in seven league boots thousands of years ago. With his giant hands he reached up in the tallest pine trees and choked the spitting mountain lion to death and devoured him raw. He outran the deer and with one blow broke its neck and devoured him raw. And it took a whole deer to fill him!*
>
> *"For a dime, the little sum of ten cents, come in and gaze upon the terrifying lineaments of the forerunner of the Java man from whom we are descended.... Come in and meet Col. Stone, the twin of Goliath, whom David slew with a slingshot. Have you forgotten your Bible? Come in and meet Col. Stone, the find of the ages...."*[49]

Ironically, the petrified man purchased by Fitzsimmons in a Denver junkyard was very likely the same hefty relic trotted out a generation before in another Colorado town. The "ape-like stone giant" was "found" near Pueblo on September 21, 1877. None other than showman P. T. Barnum appeared on the scene the very next day, offering a "big price for the stone giant," which was soon nicknamed "the Muldoon" and put on exhibit in Colorado Springs. The *Rocky Mountain News* attacked "the stone giant" as a fraud and a swindle only a week later, and stories continued for a month, with the *News* concluding near the end of October that "the Muldoon" was "neither petrified nor antique."

After thinking about it for a month, Barnum finally purchased the fake relic on October 24, 1877 and undoubtedly welcomed the free publicity from the newspaper stories that continued until December. When the scheme had run its course the Muldoon retired from public view, and was put to rest in the Denver junkyard where Fitzsimmons found it.[50]

By the end of May 1892, Soapy, too, had worn out his welcome in Creede. A delegation of law-abiding townspeople visited him to announce their intention of installing a legitimate government. In any event, Soapy's heart was no longer in Creede, and he quietly boarded the train back to Denver.

The life and death of a boomtown like Creede comes so quickly on each other's heels that every incident is reported and becomes magnified in importance. It's hard to believe that this whole trajectory took less than six months. Soapy arrived and organized the town government in February; his *Orleans Club* was running full swing in March. Joe Simons died on March 19, and the Colonel Stone incident began with the fake discovery on April 9.

In the dénouement of the boomtown, Bob Ford's premonitions proved out, as Ed O'Kelley, a distant relative of Jesse James arrived in town and on June 9 murdered Ford in a unprovoked revenge attack.

Jeff and Joe

Knowed Joe Simons? Course I did;
Knowed him 'fore he up and slid
'crost the range that wintry day;
Did he slide? Well I should say.
Not the way you mean it though,
Up the hill we toted Joe,
And we laid him 'neath the rocks,
Death had called the turn Jack Box.

'Fore he cashed in Jeff Smith came,
Asked if nothing could be done;
Jeff you see, thought well of Joe,
Had known him thirty years or so.
They'd pal'd together down below,
Worked together tooth and nail
Punchin' cattle on the trail,
Dealt the old thing, tackled bluff,
Each one blew the t'other's stuff,
And when one got in the hole,
T'other just dug up the roll;
So the boys all come to know
That Joe liked Jeff and Jeff liked Joe.

When the great excitement came
Everyone that played the game
Square or sure that could succeed,
Packed his grip and came to Creede.
Miners, merchants, maques, and marks,
Surething men and bunco sharks,
Men of money, men of greed,
Everyone fetched up at Creede.

JEFF AND JOE

And with all this human show
To the front came Jeff and Joe,
Opened up the Orleans Club*,*
Slept on tables, cooked their grub
And began to cop the dough
'Till Old Death showed up for Joe.

Jeff dropped in to see the end
Of his old time pal and friend,
For, you see, he wished to know
The last wishes of poor Joe.
"Hello Joe you're gainin' ground,"
Jeff remarked, lookin' 'round.
"Yes," Joe answered, "but the change
Soon will take me 'crost the range.

"Now, Old Boy, before I go
Just you tell me, yes or no
Did I ever throw a friend,
Didn't I stay to the end?
Through the toughest of the tough
Did I ever make a bluff?
Ever treat a poor cuss mean?
Ain't I ante'd my last bean?
Can you show me ary place
Where I've weakened in the race?
Tell me Jeff, my race is run."
And Jeff answered, "Nary one."
"Well," said Joe, "I'm glad of that,
It comes easy to stand pat,
When you know that you've done right,
Even death itself looks bright."

"Now old boy, don't preach and pray.
Keep the gospel sharks away;
'Tain't no use to call 'em late
Just to boost me through the gate;

But let the boys, all hand in hand,
A loyal true but jovial band,
Gather 'round and fall in line
And sing the Days of Auld Lang Syne;
From each bottle break the neck.
Fill each glass with Pomeroy Sec
And let each true friend drink this toast
'Here's to Old Joe Simon's ghost.'"
Jeff said, "Joe, it shall be done."
And Joe answered, "Let 'er come."

Maybe you don't think that we
Kept, in all sincerity,
Jeff's last promise to poor Joe.
Up the mountains 'round the rocks,
Came the wagon with the box;
Up the mountain, through the snow,
'Till we reached the grave of Joe.
There with heads uncovered all,
Jeff Smith opened up the hall,
Asked if anybody there
Could say Joe Simons wasn't square,
Or ever yet a wrong had done
Of Old Joe Simons, my best friend.
"Now fill your glasses, fall in line
And sing the Days of Auld Lang Syne."

They drank and sang; the pure white snow
Fell softly on the grave of Joe.
And as for Jeff, well I can say,
No better man exists today.
I don't mean good the way you do,
No not religious, only true;
True to himself, true to his friend.

Don't quit nor weaken to the end;
And I can say, if any can,
That Jeff will help his fellow man;

And here I thank him don't you see,
For kindness he has shown to me.

The Good Book says, at least I think
It says, that who so giveth drink
To the least of one of these,
The Savior he is bound to please.
But then, of course, I do not know
If this applies to Jeff and Joe.

But this I know; When all is o're
And we have crossed to t'other shore
I hope we'll stand an equal show
With sinners just like Jeff and Joe.
Billy DeVere "Tramp Poet of the Rockies"

Denver Redux

When Soapy returned to Denver in the summer of 1892, it was to a different political climate. With the *Rocky Mountain News* maintaining a steady drumbeat for reform, the police were under more pressure to at least create the impression of toughening up on organized crime. In the meantime, Soapy adroitly reestablished his position in Denver. He reopened his *Tivoli Saloon*, and was soon back at the old street corner hawking sure-thing soap for pocket money.

But it didn't take Soapy long to find trouble. On July 27, one John Culley, "Reverend" Bowers, and Soapy were arrested for fighting on the corner of Seventeenth and Market Streets. Culley, as it turns out, was the mark, and in his statement to police, he gave a classic exposition of the way the bunco game was played. The *Denver Republican* reported the game in its article, "A Sucker Refuses to Play, and the Usual Fight Follows."

> *He claimed that he was walking on the street when he made the acquaintance of Bowers. He said he was a prospector. Bowers said he had some fine specimens of ore he would like to show him, and for that purpose invited him upstairs into Smith's gambling house at Seventeenth and Market. Culley alleges that there the men behind the tables tried to induce him to gamble. He says he refused and that a row, for his benefit was immediately started. The base of operations was soon transferred by Culley to the sidewalk downstairs. During the melee he had secured an umbrella, and was using it in defending himself. He was cornered between a telegraph pole and a wagon when the officers came to his assistance and put all three under arrest.*[51]

After the arrest, Smith flatly denied his involvement. When a witness, G. R. Ford, stepped forward to place him at the scene, Smith, "reaching over Officer Riley's shoulder, struck Ford between the eyes with his fist."

Police Chief Farley, widely thought to be in cahoots with the gang, at first ordered Smith's gambling house closed, but quickly reversed his decision later in the day after hearing Smith's explanation that Culley had not been asked to play and had lost no money.

And so Soapy's career continued as he dodged the law and the law tried to find charges that would stick. On October 14, law enforcement closed in on Soapy's *Tivoli Saloon*, and then charged Soapy himself in a wine room crime.

By 1893 gambling and political corruption were widely spoken of as one and the same. Alleged corruption, bribery, and graft were features of every electoral contest. Soapy, Ed Chase, and Bat Masterson figured in the leadership of the saloon and gambling interests that regularly sold their services to whichever party needed them.[52]

Promising sweeping reform and an end to corruption, Davis H. Waite rode into the fray as a candidate for governor on the *Populist* ticket. In an inflammatory speech, he boldly proclaimed he would "fight iniquity until the blood runs as deep as the Cavalry's bridles," and was promptly nicknamed "Blood-to-the-Bridles"-Waite. Surprising many political analysts and voters alike, the Populist flood-tide swept Waite into office, propelled by possibly the most important issue in Colorado history, free silver. Little did Coloradoans know that while the Populist victory was sweet at home, the fight had already been lost on the national scene. The Populists and free silver lost decisively in 1873 when the national treasury ceased purchasing silver.

After his election, Waite waded into the battle to clean up Denver and improve its image as the capital of Colorado. As an opening salvo Waite ordered the resignation of the Denver Fire and Police Commission, widely known to be in the pay of the gambling faction. When the commissioners refused to resign, Waite threatened to call out the militia to enforce his edict. The ultimate showdown, still referred to as "The City Hall War," took place on March 15, 1894.[53]

Few thought that Waite would carry out his threat, but after the call went out to the militia on the evening of March 14, the city officials barricaded themselves in City Hall, and then, in an ironic acknowledgement of their dependent relationship on the gambling faction, called Soapy Smith to command the defense. Smith assembled an army of confidence men, bunco steerers, and denizens of the gambling halls, gathered all available weapons from local pawn shops, and detailed his men to positions in the second floor windows of City Hall along with the police and some of the fire men. Smith himself arrived with five hundred pounds of dynamite and many cases of ammunition.

The militia marched into the city and took up their positions confronting the heavily defended City Hall, with strategically positioned artillerymen and sharpshooters ready to fire. With a battering ram stationed in front of the main entrance, General Brooks called for a parlay with the commissioners. Outside town, General McCook of the regular U.S. Army was ready with seven companies of infantrymen on standby to move in and suppress the expected insurrection.

Even if Waite was fully prepared to destroy City Hall, Brooks recognized the real dangers of a violent confrontation, and refused to act without a direct order from the Governor. Instead he scrawled a message and had it hand delivered to Waite, ensconced behind bodyguards at the governor's residence, just blocks away.

"If a single shot is fired," wrote Brooks, "they will kill me instantly, and they will kill you in fifteen minutes. But if you say fire, we'll fire." Finally some of the more level headed of Denver's prominent citizens succeeded in convincing Waite to hold fire, and agree to allow the courts to settle the question. When word reached Brooks, the militia marched back to the armory, and cheers rose from police and the sports defending "their" City Hall. The threat of a real insurrection was over. Ultimately the court ordered the recalcitrant commissioners to resign, and Waite installed a new administration, putting heat on the gamblers and their establishments.

While the dramatic local battle and the ensuing city reform effort would have seemed to be reason enough for Soapy to find Denver an uncomfortable place to operate, in fact, larger forces were at work. With the defeat of the silver faction in Congress, the price of silver was in freefall, and easy money was not what it had been. Colorado fortunes had been built on silver: silver at Leadville, silver at Creede, silver at Aspen. But the fortunes of Colorado were now dependant on the price of silver, and the price of silver was dependant on mandated purchases by the U.S. Treasury for silver coins. The price of silver was a long running national political point of confrontation. And the economy of Colorado was at stake.

When the U.S. Treasury ceased purchases of silver in 1873, the resulting surplus, exacerbated by huge new discoveries, caused a steady decline in its value. With continuing effort, western "Silver" Senators managed to get the *Bland-Allison Act* passed in 1878 mandating the resumption of Treasury purchases. For the next six years, with the price of silver held constant at $1.29 an ounce, prosperity was guaranteed in Colorado.

But the prosperity of western upstarts did not benefit the eastern capitalists who advocated using the gold standard, and backed the ongoing efforts of the anti-silver forces. In response, the pro-silver factions joined farmers and labor activists to form the *Populist Party* in 1891. The first, highly idealistic platform called for free coinage of silver, the abolition of national banks, a graduated income tax, government ownership of railroads, and an eight-hour work day. In Colorado the *Populist Party* also supported the government reform efforts to end corruption, and thus earned the immediate support of the *Rocky Mountain News*. Colorado went solidly *Populist* in the fall elections in 1892, electing Davis Waite and others. Nationally however, there was a different story: anti-silver President Grover Cleveland had been returned to office. In the elation of local wins, the future dawned slowly on euphoric Coloradoans, until the price of the metal plunged to only 62 cents an ounce, less than half of its highest price Denver was thrown into a panic as major mines ceased production and ten Colorado banks failed.

When the *Sherman Silver Act* was repealed in 1893, the Treasury ceased its silver purchasing program, throwing the entire country into a depression. The final price plunge broke even millionaires like Horace Tabor. At the height of his fortune, Tabor had divorced his first wife, the hard-working but plain Augusta, and married the attractive young divorcee Elizabeth "Baby" Doe, with whom he set up a fairy-tale life in a Denver mansion. And at the height of his fame, he had even managed to get himself elected Senator. Now Tabor was flat busted, along with nearly all miners and mine owners alike.

President Cleveland and the anti-silver forces refused to provide any relief for hard-hit farmers, miners, and working people in

1894 and 1895, setting the stage for William Jennings Bryan's 1896 Populist presidential campaign, and his famous "Cross of Gold" speech.

It was the 1893 depression that really spelled the end of Soapy's high times in Denver. Editor John Arkins had sided with the Populists in the election and in the calls for reform. After the City Hall War he was incensed and turned up the heat under the con men, continuing his editorial vendetta against Soapy in earnest, through 1894. With the money in Denver all gone, the various factions began to squabble among themselves.

Soapy was dismayed. Not only had his heady control over the whole town of Creede become just a memory, but now his hold on Denver was slipping. And worst of all, brothers Lou and Sam Blonger presented the first serious challenge to his leadership on the streets. The brothers had arrived in Denver in the early 1880s and opened a saloon. They quietly added the lure of gambling to the sale of alcohol and then eased their way into control of larger underworld operations. Lou Blonger built up his political connections and became an able fixer, always with the backing of *Denver Post* owner Harry Tammen, who was his close personal friend from the early days.[54]

Soapy knew that if he left the city again, there would be no place for him to return to. But he had no choice. In 1894 and 1895 he was alternately on the road, looking for a new field of operation, or back in Denver, invariably in trouble. His relationship with the police was strained. And he again lost his temper. He was arrested for assaulting a police officer after gang member George Wilder was accused of steering a mark to a crooked poker game where he lost all his money. Three months later, four more of Soapy's steerers were in the Denver jail: W. H. Jackson, J. Anderson, "Reverend" Bowers, and Soapy's brother Bascom. Soapy was able to get them released only by agreeing that they would all leave Denver.

Frustrated at every turn, before Soapy left town he and Bascom went on a bender that would prefigure the circumstances of Soapy's classically tragic end. The Smith brothers started drinking at the *Arcade*, where the headstrong Bascom attacked gambler Johnny Hughs for no apparent reason. Then the intoxicated Smith brothers crashed through saloon after saloon, emptying their guns at the ceiling, trying to pick a fight, heaving beer kegs through the windows. Soapy managed to disappear before the police caught up with them, but Bascom was arrested and charged with murderous assault.

Over the following three years, Soapy was in so many places, and spent so much time traveling that it is difficult to establish an exact chronology. He tried his hand at establishing operations in Spokane, Pocatello, Cheyenne, Colorado Springs, Salt Lake City, and Ogden. In St. Louis he was arrested for mere vagrancy, an affront to his status in the world of con men. In New Orleans he got into more fights.

Looking for opportunity in Texas, Soapy found only more trouble. In Houston he ran into an old friend, Colonel W. R. Riddle, only to find himself in the middle of a feud between Riddle and his rival, J. O. Dalton, over the rights to operate a faro game. On December 12, 1895, before he could figure out a plan of action, Soapy found himself following Riddle into Dalton's saloon. Riddle had his gun drawn, but Dalton was waiting for him, and fired as Riddle walked through the door, killing him instantly. Soapy was stunned by what he had witnessed, but quickly followed Dalton's suggestion to get out of Houston.[55]

From El Paso, Soapy then cooked up perhaps the most bizarre, yet ambitious, scheme of his career. He traveled to Mexico and, having assumed the title of "Colonel," arranged a meeting with Porfirio Diaz, President of the Republic of Mexico. Somehow Smith had heard that Diaz was having trouble finding enough soldiers to defend his second term in office. Smith offered to raise an army of mercenaries. Always a convincing talker, Soapy easily interested Diaz, then hit him with the pitch: all Soapy needed was a small down payment of say, $10,000, to equip the new troops. But Diaz could not simply extract a roll of bills from his back pocket, like the marks in Denver. While Soapy returned to Denver, suspicious Mexican government officials checked his story and immediately discovered the bogus title, quashing the con.[56]

By the last part of 1895, there was a hint of desperation in his restless traveling. Once again he attempted to make inroads in Texas, only to be arrested in Dallas on October 12. After getting wind of the fact that the Dallas sheriff had wired the Denver authorities to inquire if Smith was wanted there, the *Denver Times* had a field day with Soapy's situation:

Jeff R. Smith, once king of the Colorado bunco steerers and past aide-de-camp to President Diaz of Mexico is now jailed as a common vagrant. This is all very pathetic.... The county authorities hardly believe it is worth while to spend money to bring Jeff Smith back. He is such a pleasant figure at a distance of six hundred miles....

Denver Times, October 12, 1895.

By now the only place in Colorado with money was Cripple Creek, where a gold strike had been made in 1891. The resulting capital-intensive hard rock mines were the saving grace of the Colorado economy. But the city fathers were on the lookout and had hired "Three-fingered" Jim Marshall, a former member of the Denver sporting crowd himself, to keep the gang members out of their town. When Soapy attempted to move into Cripple Creek at the beginning of 1896, Marshall met Soapy's train, and insured he stayed on it until it pulled out of the station again.

Soapy momentarily despaired. He felt as if the heady times, the high life, would never return. Then, as he had following the death of his friend in Creede, Soapy recovered his aplomb. He was back in Denver talking big, vowing to smoke out the Blonger Brothers. A policeman saw him start to enter the Blonger card room, but talked him out of it. Later, police asserted that Lou Blonger had been waiting for Smith with a double-barreled shotgun. (Keeping his wits about him, and his heavies handy, Lou Blonger remained as the head of the gang that ruled Denver until 1922.)

The real death knell for free silver was the discovery of more gold, first in Cripple Creek, then in Australia, the South African Transvaal, and in 1896-98 in the Yukon and Alaska. These discoveries bailed out the world monetary system: between 1895 and 1905 world gold production tripled, leading to an increased supply of money and an uptrend in the economy. And these discoveries portended glorious new opportunities for Soapy Smith.

A number of articles appeared in Denver papers, purporting to have the last word on Soapy's plans:

"Col Jefferson Randolph Smith makes his departure today"
A trio for the orient bound; The Rev. Mr. Bowers and Doctor Jackson will accompany Jeff Smith....[56]

"Denver is more or less threatened with the loss of her most prominent citizens"

Col. Jeff R. Smith, the Reverend Bowers, and Doctor W. H. Jackson have declared their intention to go to Japan.... They announce their object is a pleasure and sightseeing trip, but judging from the props they were seen carrying, they intend to be prepared for emergencies.

Fourteen packs of new cards, a dice box, and a set of "ivories"—full sets of poker chips, a small square frame covered with canvas, half shells of English walnuts, and quart bottles of good whiskey along with several boxes of fine cigars.[58]

The most definitive report on the true plans of the group appeared in the *Denver Times* on July 22. It was a letter from Soapy dated Spokane, July 14, 1897. Although the recipient had been enjoined to keep plans a secret, the letter was printed in the *Times.*

"Call out the troops: Colonel Jefferson Smith is going to the Klondyke"
"Writes to a friend here"

News reached Denver in a letter to a member of the metropolitan police department: "During a long and honorable career in Denver Col. Smith was on most amicable and friendly terms with the metropolitan police department, and the memory of these pleasant associations, he says in his letter prompts him to communicate news of his plans to the department through the medium of his favorite correspondent. Spokane, July 14, 1897":

Just preparing to set off on a new lay... I expect to be a millionaire with a biled shirt [i.e., a very white, starched shirt] on in no time at all.... I start for the Klondyke tomorrow night and before I return I propose to have more of the yellow than some people ever flopped a finger over in their palmist days.

I suppose you fellows down there have heard something about what this Klondyke business is if you have been reading the newspapers for anything but what the fire and police board is going to do with your scalps. So you will know that there is a good chance for a good talker and a petrified man in Klondyke at this stage of the game. And if I didn't say it myself, there ain't any of them that can out-talk old Jeff. What dy'e say?

We'll open up a real estate and mining office when we get there, and I'll gamble they'll tumble like tired doves.

Yank will be up there by the time I am, and Joe Bowers is already out at Seattle waiting for the word.

The only thing I AM SCARED OF IS THE FLY BULLS *[the Canadian mounted police] who* ARE *English, and they might want too much of a cut. That was the one thing I liked about Denver, the coppers never took no more than a fair divvy. If it hadn't been for others, I would of been there yet.*

Give my best to Sam Howe, for he is a square old geezer, even if he did always have it in for me. And for god sakes, don't tell 'em that you saw me.

Yours as ever,
Soapy

This is all purported to be the letter itself, but of course it may be partly fabrication. While Soapy carried on a voluminous correspondence with his associates, hints of journalistic additions in this particular missive include an excess of bragging and slang. These qualities make it read too much like what the *Denver Times* would expect Soapy to say. However, other sources confirm that he was in Spokane for a while. The *Denver Times* concluded that this was a sure indication that the Klondike craze was more than mere wind after all, "For the Colonel would never go to Alaska unless he were in a position to know exactly what he was doing."[59]

Capers and Cons in Skagway

When Soapy arrived in Skagway in mid-August of 1897, the town was a mere babe-in-arms, toddling out of the swamp at the head of the tidal flats where the Skagway River emptied into Skagway Bay and the Lynn Canal. Two hundred claim jumpers had come to town on July 29, and Captain Moore had been unable to stop them from taking over.[60]

The newly-appointed city engineer, a surveyor named Frank Reid, laid out lots in the delta between flanking mountains. Now the wide but muddy thoroughfare grandly dubbed Broadway snaked back through the forest as buildings sprang up, board shacks next to rough tents, among the stumps and remaining trees.

By mid-August, U.S. Commissioner John U. Smith and surveyor Frank Reid began to survey lots and record titles, charging $5 per lot. Members of the self-appointed town council sold 1,100 lots in two days. However, in reality, the commissioner had no authority to record such titles, as the official recorder's office was at Juneau. In the chaos that was Skagway, lot jumping was rampant and such titles did no good anyway. The reporter for the *Washington Evening Star* observed that, "For all the recording of lots, no title here is respected except squatter's rights."[61] [After the gold rush was over, Moore won his legal battle to establish his right of possession, and a settlement valued at $100,000.]

Soapy's roving eye scoped out the new town, looking for potential profits. His gaze lit on *Clancy's Saloon*, one of the first buildings along Broadway. Here was a going establishment that would fit right into his plans. Soapy went into partnership with John Clancy and began running his operations out of the saloon, with the prostitutes in their "cribs" in the back under control of his growing gang. After his disappointments of the last two years, full control was what Soapy was after, but he was secure enough to realize that it would not come all at once. One of his early moneymakers was the age-old protection racket, the basic shakedown. Soapy convinced Skagway's business owners that they needed to pay him protection money. If they agreed, his thugs would not bother them, and the gang would shield the joint from other random violence. Once Soapy was established, saloon owners had little choice but to accept the deal.

Key gang members probably arrived with Soapy, or shortly thereafter. Gang treasurer George Wilder was widely thought to have bankrolled the trip, and W. H. Jackson and the Rev. Bowers were mentioned in newspaper articles describing their departure from Denver. Young J. H. Foster, sometimes known as Slim Jim, was listed as the proprietor of the saloon known as "The Grotto," at the corner of Trail and Holly Streets, advertising as early as October 22 in the new weekly, the *Skaguay News*. Most likely he simply functioned as the owner of record for a gang-run operation. Another probable gang operation was at first called Rice's Place, operated by Jake Rice. By mid-February it was known as the People's Theater. Thugs and con men arrived two or three at a time throughout the fall and winter, gradually infiltrating the town to join the gang. Some took jobs as bartenders, while others set up their shell games on the street corners, and their gambling devices in existing saloons. Since the majority of Skagway's residents had just arrived themselves, it was not at all obvious that there was an actual gang.

The matter of law and order, or the lack of it, was apparent to all. *New York World* reporter Sylvester Scovel, one of the earliest reporters to visit Skagway, accused the commissioner of fraud in an article titled: "A POOH BAH IN SKAGUA." And sub-titled: "United States Commissioner Smith All-Powerful in That Camp."

> *The comic opera regulations of Alaska shine brightly in the whiskey question. Licensed by one United States official, saloon-keepers are selling all the fighting whiskey that the United States customs officer misses in his search of the vessels coming into port, and over all is a veritable Pooh-Bah of a commissioner whose fifty functions vie with each other in importance and impotency. It seems high time that some real government obtained in Alaska.*[62]

The sole U.S. Marshal in the region was James Shoup, stationed a few miles away in Dyea, near the foot of the Chilkoot Trail. When Shoup had to escort prisoners to Sitka or Juneau for trial, he left his nephew John N. Snook, in charge, sworn in as Deputy Marshal.

Some accounts allege that Soapy had first attempted to set up operations in Dyea during one of Shoup's absences, and had tried to bribe the twenty-one-year-old Snook to look the other way. However, Snook stood up to Soapy, and let him know directly that he had better be gone before the marshal himself returned.

Soapy found the yeasty situation in Skagway more flexible. There he confronted what seemed like a revolving door of U.S. Deputy Marshals who were to have little effect on the gang's operations.

Soapy Smith was thirty-six when he arrived in Skagway. He had been married for almost twelve years, though probably only the most trusted members of his original Denver gang were aware of it, because his wife and children lived in St. Louis. So, after looking over the town, and setting up his operations, Soapy took a trip back to the States. He stopped to visit his family in St. Louis, but the chief reason for his trip was to recruit additional talent on the West Coast. Soapy kept up a steady correspondence with old friends and associates who kept track of one another and of the business, legal, and political climate in various parts of the West. He received letters from Denver, St. Louis, Spokane, San Francisco, and as far away as Guatemala.[63]

Here, for instance, is a typical job inquiry from an eager and apparently experienced jobseeker:

Hotel Butler
Seattle, April 1st, 1898
Mr. Jeff Smith
My Dear Mr. Smith,
After you consult with Mr. Ed Byrnes, please inform me by return of mail if you have any place for an average Broad spieler and fair T.B. man. If so please write me at once here by return of mail. Please give my regards to Hughy Higgins, Ed Byrnes and other friends. Very Respectfully,
L.E. Hank.

In another instance, John W. Murphy, apparently already well connected with long-time gang member Bowers, and with John Bull and Durff, or Duffy, from Denver, wrote from Seattle, in a letter rather typical of the generally obsequious attitude Soapy inspired in his flunkeys:

Seattle, Wash. May 9, 1898
Friend Jeff,
I understand Bowers has gone to Skagway. I wrote him to Victoria and Vancouver, but have rec'd no answer. I was in good shape here to get on my feet but old Bull had me pinched on a deal that Bowers and I was in, and because I didn't turn the proceeds over to him, he had Durff swear his life against me, which caused me some trouble. Bull has lost many friends and is not in it. I will have things all right in a few days. Jeff it makes no difference what people say for or against you. I am always your friend and I hope you are doing well. I will make some money here but it wont be through the Bull click. Write me soon as you get this. I have two letters for Bowers. One from Skagway and I think it is from you. As soon as I know where Bowers is I will forward them on to him. Write by return mail. Ever your friend.
JNO. W. MURPHY Care "Horse Shoe Saloon."

Bat Masterson wrote regularly from Denver after Soapy had been drummed out, updating him on the doings of his brother Bascom, and the conditions generally:
1825 Curtis St.
Denver, Colo. Jan. 24, 1897
Friend Jeff,

Your letter from Los Angeles received. Glad to hear from you.

I supposed you were in the new camp of Randsburg. I believe you are a little like myself— "let the new camps run for other people." I do not intend to ever again go to a new camp; at least until it has demonstrated that there is something in it besides wind.

Everything is running open here, but the play is very spotted. It has got to be a piking [insubstantial] game all over town. A decent change in will attract a crowd of sufficient size to obstruct a view of the table.
Yours,
W. B. Masterson.

Con men, grifters, cardsharps, tricksters, gambling cheats, rascals, rogues, and thugs of all kinds traveled north from the Barbary Coast section of San Francisco, the skid roads, and seamy red-light districts of towns from Spokane to Denver, and from the boomtowns and cattle towns of the so-called Wild West. Soapy coordinated all of this talent and his associates found fertile fields in Alaska.

The core of the gang had been perfecting their scams and swindles in Denver for years. George Wilder, the gang's money man, arrived from Denver looking every inch the part of the rich investor from the East. The "Reverend" Charles Bowers was there, as the easy talking grip man. Van Tripplett, "Old Man Tripp," was always ready with a new disguise, and a new part to play. For the duration, he would become the experienced sourdough, ready on the beach of Skagway with his sage advice, steering the unwary directly into the clutches of the gang. "Slim Jim" Foster, still an ingénue on the confidence stage at twenty-two, had joined as a teenager in the gang's last days in Denver. New names that joined the gang in Skagway included the Moon Faced Kid, Kid Jimmy Fresh, the Lamb, the Queen, and the Blackjack. Paternally, Soapy sometimes called them all his "lambs."

By October, principal operations moved to the new "*Jeff Smith's Parlor*" on Holly Street. The new marks were most often lured into the games at Jeff's, and then simply robbed.

Soapy's main source of control continued to be the protection racket. In spite of the laws of the new territory, which prohibited the sale of alcohol, there were dozens of saloons in full operation. With the aid of his thugs, Soapy's racket was to convince the owners that he could protect them from the police. Then, with a cut of the profits, he persuaded the marshal to look the other way. He convinced those who aspired to the role of city father that without his control over the underworld characters, there would be even more violence. And of course, he trotted out his old line about only fleecing the strangers and the newcomers. As two contemporaries who saw him in action put it, "Merchants and businessmen, hungry for the lavish patronage of the gang of rogues, aided and abetted. There was a reign of terror. Honest men were intimidated. The people were cowed. It was the policy of the gang to prey upon transient travelers and leave such residents as did not oppose them unmolested. The better element became callous and submissive."[64]

The prostitutes in the back of the saloons were an important source of protection money for the gang. But one particularly courageous and sincere young woman named Molly Walsh foiled this part of Soapy's plan. Molly, an attractive young woman in her mid-twenties, arrived as a single female trying to make her way to the Klondike. On the ship from Seattle, she had met the young Rev. Robert M. Dickey, who had been sent by the Canadian missionary society to establish a church. Molly was soon a mainstay, helping the church and at the tea and crumpet society, while she obtained work at various restaurants around town. She also attended the gala masked ball held that fall for the town citizens.

All went well until Molly discovered to her horror and sorrow that a young friend of hers from her days at the Catholic school back home in St. Paul had chosen the other path, and now lay ill and dying in the back of Clancy's Saloon. Molly courageously attended her friend until her death. Then she persuaded the Rev. Dickey to hold a proper funeral in his new church. The good women of the town were at first scandalized at the notion that they should even acknowledge the existence of the prostitutes, let alone contemplate sitting amongst the working girl's compatriots. But to the edification of those who attended, Rev. Dickey preached a sermon they would not soon forget, using the story of the lost lambs.

Soon the good women of Skagway were confronting the problem head on, urging the prostitutes to give up the profession and return to their homes. Captain O'Brien, just in port with the *S.S. Shamrock*, was persuaded to provide free passage for all of the women who would agree to mend their wicked ways. A collection was taken up for their support when they reached Seattle, and with much fanfare the ship of soiled doves cast off.

But prostitution had provided the gang with much of their income, and Soapy and his male confederates were not happy with the loss of the business. Rumor had it that they blamed Molly Walsh, and Molly soon felt that her safety was threatened. She solved the problem by opening an eatery in a tent on the Canadian side of the summit of the White Pass, under the watchful eyes of the Canadian Mounties. For the rest of the winter, she cheerfully served fresh doughnuts and hot coffee to gold seekers and became a favorite of the packers.[65]

Soapy soon set up his own establishment, *Jeff Smith's Parlor*, in a

Previous Page: Jeff Smith as he appeared in Denver in the 1890s. (Denver Public Library F17094).

Above State Street, Leadville, circa 1880, in the area of the red light district. At this time Soapy was practicing his career as a shell game artist and learning the soap game. (Denver Public Library X-6528)

Top Right: Looking down 17th Street from Larimer Street toward the new Union Depot in Denver. This was the very area where Soapy operated the soap game for many years. (Denver Public Library X-22053).

Bottom Right: View of Larimer Street between 16th and 17th Streets in Denver, after 1890. A caption on the back of the photograph reads, "The two story building 2nd from left was the Arcade famous gambling den" (Denver Public Library X-23450).

ALHAM
BEER

"In my games, the player cannot win. But when he leaves, he has learned a valuable lesson—an experience of the greatest value"
Soapy Smith

Above: Gambling in a Leadville saloon. Each of the games would have been operated by a professional gambler on a franchise with the saloon owner. (Denver Public Library X 297).

"A gambler is one who teaches and illustrates the folly of avarice; he is a non-ordained preacher on the vagaries of fortune and how to make doubt a certainty"
Soapy Smith

JEFF. SMITHS PARLOR.
PARLOR
317.
LUNCH

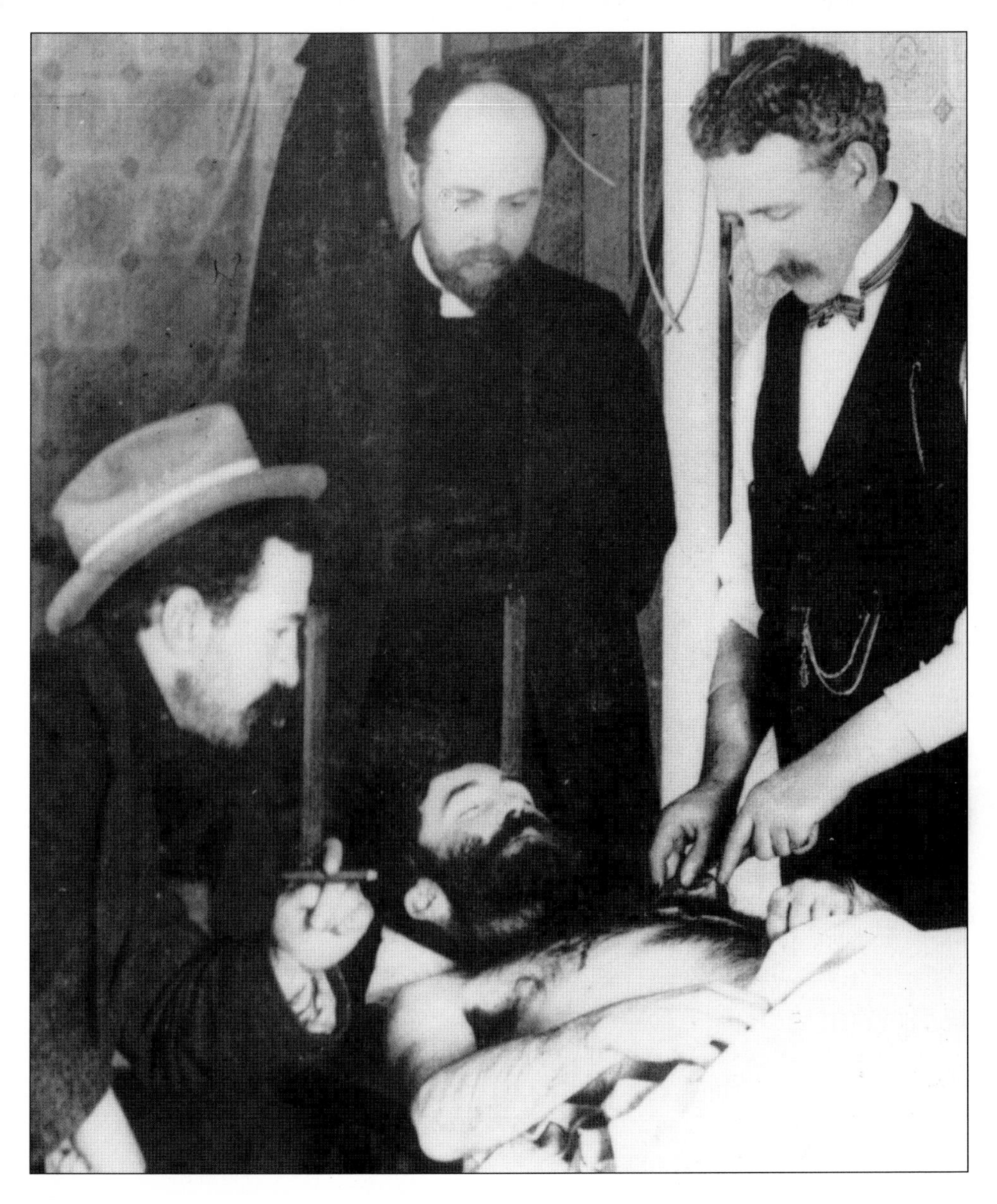

Opposite: A group of men stand in front of Jeff Smith's Parlor in the late spring of 1898. (University of Alaska Fairbanks70-58-246).

Above: Soapy's body as the coroner performs the autopsy in the morgue, one of a famous series of photos by E. A. Hegg (Yukon Archives #2687).

"There's a time to work, a time to play, and a time to die"
Soapy Smith

"Gentlemen, I should be recognized as a public benefactor! I could name many men who have renounced gambling, have been cured of avarice and cupidity and restored to mental health by taking my treatment... Praise, not censure, should be our portion"
Soapy Smith

Above: Members of the gang pose after they were rounded up, and prior to being deported back to Seattle. The man standing in the middle wearing the hat is pretending to be Soapy. (University of Alaska Fairbanks, Lulu Fairbanks #68-69-2325).

single-story frame building, a former bank on Holly Street. Soapy's genius was to cleverly fan the flames of vice and violence, and then offer himself as the solution. It wasn't long before he had insinuated himself into the heart and soul of the town, and was consolidating his control. Pretending he had a conscience, Soapy continually assured local business leaders that he alone kept the vice from escalating into violence. Meanwhile, his shell game artists and swindlers worked the streets, and his thugs in the saloons and gambling establishments enforced his protection racket. Throughout the fall, he took measures to secure his position by bribing the rudimentary law enforcement.

If anyone grew suspicious, Jeff assured him that the gang would not prey on local residents, only on hapless strangers. Or he simply offered a piece of the action. These strategies had worked in Denver. But Denver was a big city, with a seemingly endless stream of miners, cowboys, and wealthy businessmen passing through, looking for a good time. All were ripe for the picking, and none were likely to admit they had been fleeced.

On the other hand, Skagway was readying itself to receive the thousands surging north, as part of the greatest rush for gold the world had ever seen. Honest businessmen and women—from grocers and jewelers to seamstresses and sign painters, from blacksmiths to stable owners, hoped to make their own fortunes supplying goods and services to these travelers. And more importantly, in a few months the successful miners would begin to make their way back out of the Yukon with their gold dust and nuggets in canning jars and caribou skin pokes. As 1898 began, Skagway was getting a reputation as one of the roughest boomtowns ever. One prospector wrote, "I have stumbled upon a few tough corners of the globe during my wanderings beyond the outposts of civilization, but think the most outrageously lawless quarter I ever struck was Skagway.... It seemed as if the scum of the earth had hastened here to fleece, and rob, or to murder. There was no law whatsoever; might was right, the dead shot only was immune to danger."[66]

Soapy had taken precautions against bad publicity. He paid off at least one newspaper editor, who then faithfully railed against any newspaper on the West Coast that dared circulate "rumors" about violence in Skagway. When stories about violence and corruption surfaced in the Seattle papers, Soapy's shill, M. L. Sherpy of the *Skaguay News,* replied in print. He continually defended the town from so-called slanders by outsiders. On the payroll of the *Skaguay Alaskan* was William "Billy" Saportas, often described as a reporter for the *New York World*. But although Saportas and his brother E. W. were in fact from New York City, there is no evidence that Billy came to Skagway as a reporter. In fact, from the beginning of October he was the operator of the Holly House, an establishment advertised in the first edition of the *Skaguay News* and in every edition thereafter.[67]

While Soapy tried to portray the gang as simple souls who fleeced the innocent by not completely unlawful means, the atmosphere soon brought more violent activity. By spring, the action in Skagway attracted many common criminals who would just as soon attack travelers on the trail. Those who did not give up their wallets peacefully were knifed, shot, or knocked out. The situation soon spiraled out of Soapy's control, though he made valiant efforts to maintain his position.

Skagway Fights Back

Officers of the steamer Noyo from Skagway today reported conditions of lawlessness at Skagway as beyond description. Soapy Smith and his gang are in full control. Law abiding people do not dare say a word against them. Hold-ups, robberies, and shootings are part of the daily routine. Eight dead bodies were picked up on White Pass on Feb. 15.[67]

Seattle, February 25, 1898

Blackmailing Liars
A lot of Dastardly Bastards hired to run Down Skagway
Not a word of truth in what they utter Skagway the most Peaceable city in the North.

Daily Alaskan, O.W. Dunbar, Editor, February 28, 1898[69]

"Get it while the getting is good." As October gave way to November in Skagway cold winds blew down from the passes and right through the canvas tents, and the hastily built rough frame houses and saloons. Fall in Skagway had been full of excitement and anticipation with reporters from around the world collecting local color. But most people decamped before the deepest part of winter set in. Anyone who had the means would have left Skagway that winter. Soapy returned from his vacation in the States just in time to take control of a situation that threatened the delicate balance in the fledgling town. It all started on January 31, when a young man named Andy McGrath and an unknown young woman went out for a drink to the Klondike Saloon and the gambling hall located upstairs from the variety theater run by Jacob Rice. This was most likely another business controlled by the gang. The full account appeared in the *Seattle Post-Intelligencer* on February 6.

According to the paper, McGrath and the young woman entered the Theater and had some drinks. Shortly after, McGrath claimed that his liquor had been doped and that he had been robbed of $140. McGrath's charges provoked a general fight in which McGrath was badly beaten by Fay, the upstairs bartender in the Theater, assisted by several attachés of the theater. McGrath wanted revenge and went out into the street for the purpose of getting a gun and returning to finish the fight. The first man he met was U.S. Marshal Rowan. Rowan was on the way downtown to get a doctor for his wife who was in labor. Rowan agreed to go to the theater and act as pacifier. When Rowan and McGrath entered the theater, McGrath pointed to Fay, saying 'there's the man.' He then took off his coat and struck at Fay with his fist. Fay drew his revolver and fired, the bullet striking McGrath in the groin. He dropped to a chair with a groan. Rowan turned to pull his revolver from his hip pocket, when Fay fired again, the bullet striking Rowan in the stomach, Rowan recoiled, but did not fall, and reached the street where a friend found him and took him to a doctor's office a block distant.

After the shooting, Fay escaped through the back door of the theater. On Monday afternoon T. M. Ward went to Rice, proprietor of the hall, and demanded the surrender of Fay. He represented to Rice that it was absolutely necessary in order to prevent a riot. Rice finally consented and Fay was turned over to Ward, who placed him in safe-keeping.

A committee of twelve citizens was appointed to consider the case to give Fay a trial and mete out justice. Another committee of ten was appointed to guard Fay.[70]

Of course, there was still no telegraphic communication between Skagway and the outside world. News of the event reached Seattle with arriving passengers on the steamer *Seattle*, a trip that took about five days. So, the February 6 account in the Seattle newspapers ended with what was known at the time of the ship's departure from Skagway, and readers in the city were left with the assumption that Fay had been lynched, and that Mrs. Rowan and the baby had died from the shock of Rowan's death.

In fact, it was Soapy who had stepped in to spirit Fay away to safekeeping. Did he gallantly and selflessly save Fay from vigilante justice? Or was he acting in his familiar role of "fixer," saving one of his own? The controversy itself illustrates the success of one of Soapy's major tactics: obfuscation, or creating enough confusion in the mind of ordinary citizens that they came to believe that the truth could not be known. In service of this mission, Soapy's defenders at the newspapers sought to downplay the murders, and emphasize Soapy's role in keeping order.

Editorializing on its front page, the *Seattle Post-Intelligencer* reminded its readers on February 6 that early in the Klondike rush, many had predicted that chaos would ensue at Lynn Canal's ports:

> *The present condition of affairs at Skagway and Dyea has been predicted by well-posted men who have watched the mad rush of fortune hunters to the north. On this tide of humanity have floated many of that class of people who live off the weakness of others. The gambler, the confidence man and the harlot all have been represented... During the height of the migration northward last fall, the confidence men, crooks and dangerous characters were in abundance. "Soapy" Smith whose career is well known in Seattle, worked at his calling in broad day on the Skagway trail from morning to night and when he returned in the winter, it was with a wallet bulging with bills. The trouble with Alaska as pointed out in the report of Gov. Brady has been a dearth of law and a famine of authority with which to enforce such laws as apply to that territory.*[71]

The fact is, many people were aware of the problems in Skagway. From the beginning of the rush, there had been a lack of either federal law enforcement, or the political means to elect a local government with legitimate powers of law enforcement. It was this great gap that Soapy and his minions spotted and rushed into. S. H. Graves, president of the *White Pass and Yukon Route*, emphasized this in a report to the British backers in London:

> *There was no law under which any municipal government could be organized, nor was there any Federal law, or courts, or police, or authority. The only representative of the Federal government was an official known under the imposing title of "Deputy United States Marshal." He was in fact in league with the criminal element which in the circumstances described had things all their own way. The criminal element, though numerous, were in the minority. They had the advantage of being thoroughly organized and armed, and skillfully led by a man name "Soapy" Smith, who was the uncrowned king of Skagway. He was not a constitutional monarch, but his word was all the law there was.*[72]

The events surrounding the Rowan and McGrath murders prompted renewed efforts from Skagway citizens who had secretly formed a vigilance committee. They immediately drafted a petition to be sent to the War Department requesting the imposition of martial law. The petition arrived in Seattle with a representative of the committee, Dr. Rufus Smith, and was printed on Monday, February 7:

> *We the undersigned citizens and business men of Alaska respectfully petition and set forth:*
>
> *That there is an extraordinary condition of affairs existing at and near Dyea and Skagway, Alaska, which calls for prompt attention from the proper authorities. As a result of the recent discoveries of gold in and near Dawson N.W.T. Canada during the past two years there....*
>
> *In view of the fact that there is not local civil government in the territory of Alaska and no one with sufficient authority to enforce the laws of the land, much less to prevent crime and disorder, and in view of the large number of the undesirable and criminal class who are now flocking to our community to prey upon the unwary and innocent pilgrim, and in order to have some one with sufficient authority and in sufficient numbers to prevent disorder and blockades on the trails leading to lakes Lindeman and Bennett and to protect the property of citizens of the United States: We the undersigned petition that immediate action be taken by the proper authority:*
>
> *And believing this to be an extraordinary emergency, we believe that martial law should be declared in all this part of Alaska comprising the communities of Dyea and Skagway and the trails leading there from to the international boundary. And that sufficient troops, no less than 300 be immediately dispatched to these points to enforce the laws and preserve order.*[73]

In a front page article accompanying this petition in the *Post-Intelligencer*, the editors concurred with the request for martial law and went on to predict again that without some action by the authorities, there would be serious trouble before the rush was over:

> *The present situation is so grave, and the future is so sure to increase its perils, that citizens of Alaska have appealed to the war department to declare martial law. The request should be complied with at once,*

or there should be put through congress without delay legislation that will empower the people there to organize a local civil government and administer public affairs in due form of law.[74]

They pointed out that the citizens had attempted to form a local government, but that absent any real legal powers it was unstable and uncertain. They understood that among the thousands about to descend on the small town were a large proportion of the criminal element so obvious in Seattle, Port Townsend, and other Western towns already.

They were certain to make a great deal of trouble the editors contended, and it was not likely that a vigilance committee would be able to repress them effectually. They could intimidate these lawless elements only by a display of superior force, fearlessness, and determination; by a constant enforcement of the law of might.

Indeed, bunco artists, confidence men, and gamblers were a common denominator in the West. They operated in all the major cities, and all of the major boomtowns, big or small. Usually it was more trouble to get rid of them than to allow them to quietly coexist with law-abiding elements. And, fortunately, they often moved on to greener pastures. In an article titled "Crooks run out of Town," the *San Francisco Chronicle* reported:

The Klondike boom has done more for San Francisco than merely to increase the volume of business.... It has, directly aided by the Police Department, sent as fine a lot of crooks as ever jointed a jimmy or cracked a crib to other fields where while the picking may not be so rich the chances of capture are considerably lessened. Seattle is now the hunting ground of any number of these thugs, while the rest are scattered in Tacoma and Victoria, B.C.

At the time of the Christian Endeavor Convention here last July, San Francisco was the stamping ground for more desperate characters who imagined the world owed them a living than had gathered in any one place on this coast for many years....victims [are] reported daily at headquarters of the operations of short card men, flim-flammers, and other of the genus bunco.[75]

Further emphasizing the surging power of the gambling fraternity, the *Chronicle* reported on February 8, in a special dispatch from Tacoma:

> *A gambling syndicate of San Francisco and Tacoma gamblers and sporting men is now carrying out extensive plans that have been in contemplation since October. Gambling-houses have been opened in Tacoma and Seattle. Next week, the largest gambling establishment in Alaska will be in full swing at Wrangell under the syndicate's management. One of their men is operating at Rampart City on the Yukon this winter, and as early as possible houses are to be opened at St. Michael and Dawson.*[76]

The syndicate had invested $25,000 in its expansion plans and was sending an agent to New York to raise another $75,000.

Moving frequently from place to place, the members of the gambling fraternity were well positioned to assess advantageous odds between one locale and another. They formed an extensive network that traded information on favorable conditions for gambling. The major factors they looked for were a lack of governmental control and easily bribed law enforcement. While newer towns nearly always fit this model, major cities tolerated gambling to a greater or lesser extent in certain districts, and a favorable political climate could result in a fortuitous atmosphere for the thugs.

The Seattle Post-Intelligencer was well aware that a vigilance committee was the obvious, and in fact only possible response to the influx of the criminal element in the absence of any legally empowered, law-enforcement entity.

Perhaps Soapy knew the fine line he walked in Skagway. As long as he could control overt violence, especially against Skagway's more permanent residents, he might maintain the illusion of his position as a benevolent dictator of Skagway. However, undoubtedly he knew that if violence escalated, he risked a backlash from Skagway citizens, who were already meeting. On the other hand, the citizens' committee knew it was dangerous to criticize either Soapy or the gang in public, or even in private, for fear that one might be addressing the gang itself. The gang included a spy network that extended into every walk of life in Skagway. By infiltrating every meeting called to address the problem, they managed to hijack public opinion to their cause. Even at the end, no one was ever sure just who belonged to the gang.

While Soapy tried to portray his "lambs" as simple souls who fleeced the innocent by not necessarily unlawful means, in fact many common criminals had also moved in. In the end, Soapy could not control the actions of all the thugs in the town. He must have known that no matter what he promised, in reality, the situation was already out of his control.

It was only on February 8 that citizens of Seattle learned that, in fact, Fay had not been lynched, and Rowan's young wife had not died in the tragedy. Instead she was now a young widow. However, the *Post-Intelligencer* also reported that Fay's supporters, led by Soapy, "threatened that if Fay was lynched they would use their guns." Smith stated that there were 205 gang members and if Fay was lynched, there would be some shooting. Fay was thus allowed to go to the jail in Sitka to await a trial. (He was eventually acquitted on reason of self-defense.)

Finally the federal government sat up and took notice. If Alaska was to prosper, its residents must be allowed to walk the streets in safety. News reached Seattle on February 9, that following a presidential cabinet meeting in Washington, D.C., U.S. troops were ordered north, "for purposes of preserving order and protecting life and property." Two companies of the Fourteenth Infantry were to go to Dyea, and two companies to Skagway. Of course the troops were in reality still in Seattle awaiting transportation, and meanwhile dire reports reached Seattle every day. On February 11, headlines trumpeted, "Lawless element rules in Skagway, Flagrant crimes of daily occurrence. Good men outnumbered."

February 12 brought the report that a vigilance committee was being organized to drive the toughs from Skagway while they awaited the arrival of the *U.S. Wheeling* with infantry companies A and G, along with a description of the inquest, which called into question the loyalty of Commissioner John U. Smith. He was accused of failing to produce witnesses for the inquest.[77]

Meanwhile, the *Seattle Post-Intelligencer* had previously noted (on January 23) that Seattle citizens were attempting to bring charges against Commissioner Smith:

A warrant is out for the arrest of United States Commissioner John U. Smith, Skaguay, on five charges: soliciting bribe, receiving a bribe, felony, and malfeasance in office. Dr. Hornsby, a member of the Skaguay council, has filed three affidavits covering these charges with Judge Johnson of the United States District Court. The affidavits are sworn to by Skaguay businessmen. The names of the prosecutors and details of the charges had not been made public when the Seattle *left Skaguay.*

Curiously, the *Seattle Post-Intelligencer* never followed up on the charges against Smith in the Seattle District Court, relying instead,on the reports from Skagway. And, in hints of what was to come, the paper noted, "Before filing the charges Dr. Hornsby told [Soapy] Smith what he intended to do." Soapy's response was characteristic of gang tactics. "Smith thought the charges should be first investigated by a committee of citizens." This was the exact gambit that the gang did follow, after the double murders, using the "committee" to stall for time so they could get Fay out of town.

For the next week, fear of the vigilance committee kept things quiet. The committee was "made up of some of the best citizens of Skagway, and has given out that the next man to make a gun play will be hanged [i.e., lynched]." To complicate matters, news also circulated that Skagway was suffering an outbreak of meningitis.

The fragile quiet was broken when, in a shooting fray in front of the Whitehorse Saloon, Tom Ryan, a purported gang member, shot and wounded an unnamed newcomer. Meanwhile, Mike Quinlan, formerly a detective in Minneapolis, was appointed Deputy Marshal in Skagway, replacing the slain Rowan. "Strenuous efforts are being made to break the ring rule of Soapy Smith and his gang. It is said that Soapy cleared $40,000 previous fall with his shell game on the trail and so far, he 'runs' Skagway to suit himself."[78]

The *Post-Intelligencer* published a letter from George A. Brackett, dated Skagway, February 27, which showed that Soapy had plenty of sheep to fleece during the winter. Brackett reported that he had been packing and sledding with horses and oxen over the White Pass Trail to Bennett for a month without missing a day, and that two thousand other stampeders were moving their goods over it. However, he noted, little had passed over the Chilkoot, and one hundred tons were cached in the snow at the summit.

Following the McGrath-Rowan murders, the vigilantes in town became emboldened to publicly challenge Soapy and his organization. These men reportedly included Tanner, Major J. F. A. Strong, a future governor of Alaska, Rev. R. M. Dickey, Frank Reid, and according to Dickey, Skagway Bill Fonda, and Captain Jack Crawford. Fonda and Crawford both had previous experience with vigilante justice in the mining camps of California, where miners' meetings typically held court in the absence of any others.[79]

The promised troops arrived in the first week of March. They pitched their tents in the "suburbs" of Skagway, about a mile from the center of the business district, on snow and ice. Notices were posted March 8, warning that all gambling rooms and sure thing games must be closed by one o'clock the following day. Both companies of troops marched into Skagway from their camp on the deadline, and enforced the order, closing all the saloons and gambling halls, with Soapy's faction threatening vengeance.[80]

Meanwhile, inbound miner H. Bean was murdered on the White Pass Trail, shot at close range. The military authorities supposed that the motive had been robbery, but that the murderer had been scared off before searching the body. This was one of a number of incidents that prompted the vigilance committee to take public action.

A second meeting of the "Committee of 101" was held shortly after, at which the vigilantes drafted and posted another notice:

WARNING

A warning to the wise should be sufficient. All confidence men, bunco, and sure thing men and all other objectionable characters are notified to leave Skagway and the White Pass Road immediately and to remain away. Failure to comply with this warning will be followed by prompt action.

Signed, "101"

Soapy's faction met the same night, and responded boldly, announcing his own "committee," but not giving a precise name to it until later.

WARNING

The body of men styling themselves "101" are hereby notified that any overt act committed by them will promptly be met by the law abiding citizens of Skagway, and each member and his property will be held responsible for any unlawful act on their part, and the Law and Order

> *Society, consisting of 317 citizens, will see that justice is dealt out to its fullest extent as no blackmailers or vigilantes will be tolerated.*
> *Signed, "The Committee"* [81]

Here is Soapy's method of obfuscation at its finest, at the very least providing the cover of "law and order" for those who chose to condone or just ignore his depredations.

The *San Francisco Examiner* reported on the troops on March 16, 1898, "Troops Rule at Skagway," with the article datelined Victoria, March 15. According to this report, the military was confident that the gambling rooms would stay closed, and that they would be able to rid the town of the undesirable element. The gambling houses were still closed when the *Islander* sailed with this report.

This news occupied column inches of papers in Seattle, San Francisco, Denver, and elsewhere; places whose readership were kept abreast of any news related to the Klondike Gold Strike. Then, on February 16, came news that the American battleship *Maine* had been blown up and sunk while moored in the Havana harbor. Suddenly, petty crime in far-off Skagway was yesterday's news, as reports about the *Maine* disaster and possible culprits occupied front pages for the next week. The possibility of war soon became clear.

The Way of the Transgressor

Tensions only increased as spring came to the little outpost at the end of the Lynn Canal. Every day brought new reports of overloaded ships departing Seattle, Victoria, and San Francisco with thousands of gold seekers heading for Skagway and Dyea as way stations on their journey to the Klondike.

"Hundreds sail for Alaska: *Australia's* Decks were Crowded," reported the *San Francisco Chronicle* on February 22. The paper reported that three hundred had boarded at San Francisco, and another four hundred would board in Seattle. Just the next day, the same paper reported on the departure of the *Excelsior* and the *Humboldt*, carrying between them four hundred passengers, and "the usual number of dogs." On the 26th it was those on the *Pueblo* who "Sail Away in Search of Gold," accompanied by "good-by shoutings [sic] mingled with the barking of dogs."

In Alaska, businessmen in the twin ports of Dyea and Skagway, gateways to their respective trails, staged their active competition for the new gold seekers with huge advertisements in the Seattle and San Francisco newspapers. The Skagway entrepreneurs were backing the new Brackett Wagon Road with comparatively easy grades still under construction by George Brackett to improve the route over the White Pass. George Brackett was carrying on a very public debate in the Post-Intelligencer, with letters to Hugh Wallace. Brackett attacked Wallace as president of the "alleged Chilkoot Railroad & Transportation Company." Brackett did not want competition from Wallace and other methods of transportation. However, the days of his wagon road were numbered; construction began on the White Pass and Yukon Railroad on May 27.

Meanwhile, businessmen in Dyea tried to compete, continually referring to the White Pass Trail as the Dead Horse Trail, and banking on the newfangled Chilkoot tramways, a freight hauling system similar to a modern ski lift, which was to solve the problem of that awe inspiring, forty-five degree pitch just before the summit of the Chilkoot Trail. Businessmen, shop owners, hoteliers, restaurateurs, and packers had spent the whole winter preparing and waiting.

Tension was building in the jerry-built city on the inlet. In addition to the predations of the gang, residents had to deal with the dismal lack of sanitation. Garbage and animal bones lay everywhere, and there were only four public toilets in the entire town. Drinking water had to be taken from holes in the river ice. The unsanitary conditions precipitated a dangerous epidemic of spinal meningitis. Hospital facilities were inadequate and primitive.[82]

By April, Skagway was in the beginning of a tidewater spring, with the creeks flowing, and flowers beginning to bloom, even as the icy grip of winter held fast to the passes and trails in the mountains above and beyond the town. Indeed, thousands of *argonauts* arrived in April and May. While thousands of gold seekers successfully made their arduous way up the trails, built crude boats on the shores of Lake Bennett, and waited for the ice to go out of the headwaters lakes before floating down the Yukon to Dawson City, the warm weather also brought tragedy. On April 3 at noon, warming conditions led to a major avalanche on the Chilkoot Trail. The local Tlingit packers had warned cheechakos of the dangerous snow conditions that day, but many did not listen and had headed up the trail with their packs as usual that morning. Sixty-four poor souls were dug out dead, but many others were probably never found. There were rumors that Soapy's gang robbed the bodies in the temporary morgue set up at Dyea. The incident added to the tensions on the two trails. However, if additional trouble accompanied this influx, it was not reported in the West coast papers, preoccupied as they were with the Spanish-American War.

By late spring, a new preoccupation suddenly dawned on the Skagway businessmen who had now invested so much in their enterprises. Soapy Smith had promised over and over again that the gang would prey only on the newcomers, the strangers, the travelers. As long as the travelers were those hapless gold seekers making their way from south to north, the great majority of businessmen tolerated the gang's activities or persuaded themselves that things were not as bad as the Seattle and San Francisco papers reported.

But soon, those who had actually found gold in the Klondike would start to make their way south from Dawson: they would travel up the Yukon, through the lakes, and back out over the passes to Skagway. These were the men and women with real money, who had a stake in the North, and might be customers for many years. Now the businessmen really had something to lose.

The magnitude of what was at stake perhaps became painfully clear to Skagway's resident entrepreneurs when the Canadian government made elaborate plans to transport $150,000 in Queen's customs duties out of the Klondike. Fearful of skullduggery on the trail, the Mounties carefully planted the story that Mounted Police Inspector Zachary Taylor Wood was being transferred to Calgary. Acknowledging the Smith gang's control of the White Pass Trail, they decided to send Wood out with the gold via the Chilkoot Trail to Dyea, and then transport Wood and the gold by private boat to a waiting ship at the Skagway dock.

In spite of the Canadians' efforts at keeping this plan secret, the news leaked to the gang. A small skiff full of Soapy's brigands actually had the nerve to approach the gold-bearing, Mounted Police boat outside of Skagway's harbor. Sergeant Pringle and Constable Chalmers of the Mounties leveled their carbines at the would-be robbers, who wisely rowed off. Then in a technical violation of U.S. sovereignty, which everyone seems to have agreed to overlook, a squad of armed Royal Navy reservists from the ship guarded Skagway's wharf while the gold was transferred to the steamer *Tartar*. His bluff called, Soapy merely invited Inspector Wood to visit the town.[83]

If Soapy's minions were as brazen as to try to attack the Mounties themselves, what would happen to a small pack train of a few men or the single prospector returning from his claims?

In fact, the gang was already preying on lone prospectors returning from Dawson. For instance, prospector and miner Ed Lung was returning from the Klondike with a sizable poke of gold when he stopped at the White Pass Hotel at Porcupine Hill. Spotted by a member of the gang, he was asked to deliver a letter to Mr. Y. M. Hopkins, care of Jeff Smith's Parlor on Holly Street. Hopkins was Yea Mow Hopkins, the former bodyguard for members of one of San Francisco's infamous *Tongs*, and now one of the heavies for the gang. Trust was a commodity that was much admired and talked of among veterans of the California Gold Rush, and in reminiscences of Yukon prospectors, and willingness to do favors for unknown strangers was an aspect of that system of trust. So Lung gamely carried the letter down the trail and delivered it, which immediately targeted him as a mark. Hopkins in turn invited him to enjoy a round of drinks with his friends at the bar. "Lung was immediately surrounded by Hopkins' friends who refused to let him leave. Realizing that a trap was closing in on him, he made a desperate dash for the front door, and succeeded in escaping to the waterfront."[84]

Once the news of a few prospectors' bad experiences filtered back to Dawson City, no amount of harping by the coastal town's newspapers defending its reputation or the safety of its trails would save the future of Skagway. If these men thought Skagway too dangerous, and decided to take other routes with their gold, Skagway's future was ruined.

While the town lived on edge, distraction came in the form of preparations for the war against Spain. Of course Soapy managed to turn even this event into a publicity stunt for himself. On March 19 he wrote to President McKinley in Washington, offering the services of his newly formed *Skagway Military Company*, also known as *Company A, First Regiment of National Guard of Alaska*. The men were ready to train and fight in Cuba, Soapy said. The only reply he actually received was an acknowledgement of his letter, signed by the President's secretary. Soapy naturally exaggerated the story, allowing word to spread that he had received a letter signed by Secretary of War Russell Lager, commissioning him a Captain of Volunteers. Soapy backed up this story by actually producing the commission papers, which he showed to prospector Harry Suydam. Although Suydam later concluded the papers were forged, Soapy once again had created enough confusion to convince most of Skagway of the legitimacy of his "patriotic" endeavor. [85]

Soapy enthusiastically recruited and trained his new militia for service in the Spanish-American War. To demonstrate their prowess to the whole town, he staged a grand parade on May 1. Soapy rode out on his dappled grey horse in front of his troops. There was much cheering and flag waving, and the event was accompanied by flattering speeches from dignitaries, some of whom later said they were coerced.

On May 29 the town woke up to the report of a "most atrocious and mysterious murder." Mulatto prostitute Ella D. Wilson had been viciously murdered in her own bed in her little cabin on Holly Street the night before and a large trunk containing money had been broken into.[84] Of course, as with most of Skagway's crimes, the nefarious Deputy Marshal Taylor took charge of the investigation, and nothing more was heard about it. Meanwhile, Mattie Silks, the notorious Denver madam, had traveled to the Klondike earlier in the spring with some of her girls. On her return to Denver, Silks bragged to the press that she had cleared $38,000 in ninety days. However, the picture of her northern business trip grew grimmer when she later reported that on her stop in Skagway as she was exiting the country she had been threatened with murder. Far from simply ignoring the crime, Marshal Taylor was guilty of actual complicity, Mattie Silks claimed:

> *Mattie reported that she occupied a room in the* Occidental Hotel *adjoining one that served as an office for the marshal. Only a partition of thin boards separated the two rooms, and she stated that the night after the murder she heard Marshal Taylor, Soapy Smith, Bill Tanner, and Bowers, talking in Taylor's office while dividing up the money.*[87]

Not only did Silks come to understand that the money being divided on the other side of the wall was the property of Ella Wilson, Silks also claimed to have heard the cohorts plot to kill her in the same way they had killed Ella. Silks and her entourage hastened to board the next ship out of town. The incident might have yielded some hints of what was to come, but Soapy's paid defenders at the papers steadfastly denied the assertion. "Little as we believed it at the time," the *Skaguay News* admitted later, "it now looks as though the story told by Mattie Silks was true."[88]

No matter. At the time of the murder, citizens were again distracted from solving the crime as the town became more and more crowded, burgeoning into a city of fifteen thousand persons and sixty-one saloons.

As the Fourth of July approached, providing yet another occasion for showy community celebration, townsfolk were caught up in preparations for a great parade. The parade included: "a children's float featuring the Goddess of Liberty; Members of Clubs,

Societies and Secret Orders; Bicyclists, including Ladies and Gents; the *Skaguay News Boys Association*; floats representing the local trades and mechanics; appearances by the members of the Chilkat, Pyramid Harbor, and Haines Mission Tlingits," and more. For the fourth and last division, Soapy rode on his dapple grey gelding at the head of his *First Regiment of Alaska Militia*, followed by a float depicting the *U.S. Man-of-War*, and J. H. Brooks' pack train. As the caboose to the parade, young Frank Clancy, dressed as Uncle Sam in a costume made by his mother, rode on a wagon bed with a bald eagle in a chicken wire cage, decorated with bunting and six American flags. When it was time for the day's oratory, there was Soapy seated on the dais with Governor Brady and the other dignitaries.[89]

The bald eagle, symbol of America's freedom, and Soapy's military plans later became an emblem long remembered by Skagway residents as one of the icons of Soapy's treachery. Some of Soapy's boys had found the eagle and they kept it caged in the backyard of *Jeff's Parlor.* [90] The gang members used it as one of their lures, enticing the hapless or gullible into the yard surrounded by a high fence, where they were tricked into participating in other games, or simply robbed.

Four days later a successful, but hapless, prospector named John Douglas Stewart, returning from the Klondike with nearly three thousand dollars worth of gold dust in his caribou skin poke, made his way down the White Pass Trail and into Skagway. Gang members lured him into the *Parlor's* yard "to see the eagle," and then mugged and robbed him. According to the *Skaguay News* of July 8, "Rev." Bowers enticed Stewart into the yard of *Jeff's Place* on Holly Street, on pretext of exchanging the gold at a favorable rate. There, two gang members lay in wait. The three overpowered Stewart and wrested from him the sack of gold worth $2,670. In their defense, the crooks could offer only that Stewart had been lured into a crooked card game where he lost all of his money.

Stewart, cheated out of his hard-won gold, complained to the authorities—in this case Marshal Taylor. When, after some hours, he perceived that the Marshal was making no efforts to intervene, Stewart told his story to anyone who would listen, and word quickly spread to some of the prominent citizens who were involved with the vigilance committee. The citizens of Skagway were finally moved to collective action. Again according to the *Skaguay News*, these influential citizens, outraged that such a flagrant robbery should have been committed in broad daylight, sought out Soapy, and informed him that the gold must be returned.

Soapy, stalling for time, promised to return the gold. From Soapy's response, and later actions, it seems clear that he was already on edge, aware that the gang was out of his control, and that the town's patience was at an end. It seems also that many of Soapy's followers could see the writing on the wall. M. L. Sherpy, who had steadfastly defended Soapy all those months in the *Skaguay News*, now turned against him. As a first-person observer, his accounts in the *News* on the following July day offer the most complete version of events.

> *During the earlier part of the excitement, Smith partially promised several men, including the writer, that, in case there was no "roar" made in the papers, the gold would be returned by 4 o'clock, last evening, and that his influence would be used to prevent his men from in any way interfering with returning Klondikers in the future.*

Of course, since perhaps two hundred thugs were in town, and Soapy could not control all of them, his promise to use his influence was, in any case, a hollow promise, and probably everyone knew it, including Soapy. In fact, Soapy began to drink heavily at that point, and seemed, in an echo of his final spree in Denver, to have already abdicated responsibility, in spite of his promises. Sherpy continues:

> *The promise was not kept however, nor was the gold returned. On the contrary Smith began to drink heavily, and talk in a rash defiant manner. When told by a news representative that unless the gold was returned there would be trouble, Smith replies, "By ____, trouble is what I am looking for.*

The gold was not returned, public indignation increased until at eight o'clock it had reached fever heat. Cool heads prevailed, however, and no outward demonstrations were made. However, there was an ominous look worn by several hundreds of men, including the best of Skaguay's citizens, which plainly said, "sure-thing men must go."[91]

On July 8, the good citizens of Skagway convened their vigilance committee at a mass meeting at *Sylvester's Hall.* While Sherpy claimed "the space was not adequate to accommodate the crowd," other sources imply that the group could not be sure the meeting was not infiltrated by Soapy's spies.[93] In any case, they elected Thomas Whitten of the Golden North Hotel chairman, and then adjourned the meeting, to re-form at the end of the newly constructed Juneau Company Wharf at the end of Runnalls Street (today known as State Street). Here, they thought, they would have a better chance of controlling attendance. This time, the group fully intended to rid Skagway of the "lawless element."

Four trustworthy men, Frank H. Reid, Jesse Murphy, Capt. J. M. Tanner, and John Landers, were appointed to guard the approach to the dock. Soapy Smith knew full well that the townspeople were determined to drive him out, and he knew they were meeting on the wharf. By the time he appeared at the entrance to the causeway, carrying a Winchester rifle, he had been drinking for many hours. Soapy was no brave gunfighter in the tradition of the West. As we have seen, he only bet on a "sure thing." Typically, he never laid a hand on his victims; he surrounded himself with a staff of thugs paid to do his dirty work. When provoked to physical violence, as he had been in the incident with Colonel Arkins in Denver, he preferred to strike first. But this time, all of the gang had deserted him, and he seemingly had no choices. The suave rationalizer had painted himself into a corner from which there was no retreat.

When Soapy appeared at the narrow entrance to the dock between nine and ten in the evening, it was Frank Reid who challenged him. Reid, a big imposing man of 54, was an old hand in the West. He had worked as a surveyor and engineer, and he had fought Indians during the Piute War in Oregon, where he was also a schoolteacher. Soapy answered Reid's challenge by raising the barrel of his gun to strike him. Reid grabbed the gun, pushing the barrel down towards the ground, but it was too late. Soapy and Reid fired nearly simultaneously at point blank range. The ball from Soapy's Winchester struck Reid in the groin, passing through the right hip. Of the two or three shots Reid fired from his revolver, one struck Soapy in the heart, killing him instantly, as both fell in a pool of blood on the dock. Some called it suicide.

Editor Sherpy had been a staunch defender of Skagway, castigating Seattle papers that had dared to hint, in the wake of the Rowan-McGrath double murders in February, that bad elements might be in control of the town. Sherpy's attitude changed completely following this encounter with Soapy:

> *At nine o'clock last night, a meeting was started in Sylvester's Hall, but the space being inadequate to accommodate the crowd, an adjournment was taken to the Juneau dock, where at a point half way to the warehouse, a meeting was called to devise ways and means for ridding the city of the lawless element which for sometime has infested it. The meeting was called to order by J. T. Hayne, foreman of the News Office, who suggested the election of a chairman, Thomas Whitten of the Golden North hotel being chosen. The chairman appointed a committee of four, Frank H. Reid, Jesse Murphy, J. M. Tanner, and Mr. Landers, to guard the approach to the dock in order that no objectionable characters might be admitted to disturb the deliberations of the meeting. It was while this committee of four was stationed at the end of the dock that Jeff Smith appeared carrying a Winchester rifle in his hands. He walked straight up to Reid and with an oath, asked what he was doing there, at the same time striking at him with the barrel of the gun. Reid grabbed the gun in his left hand as it descended, pushing it down towards the ground, and drawing his revolver with his right hand at the same time. When the point of the rifle was close against Reid's right groin, Smith pulled the trigger. The ball passed clear through and came out through the lower part off the right hip. At about the same time Reid fired two or three shots in rapid succession, one of which pierced Smith's heart, another striking one of his legs. Smith also fired a second shot, striking Reid in the leg. Both men fell at about the same time, "Soapy" Smith stone dead, and City Engineer Reid dangerously, perhaps mortally wounded.*
>
> Skagway News special edition, *July 9, 1898.*

After bystanders carried Reid to the offices of Dr. Moore, and Smith's bloodied corpse to the undertaker, Skagway's citizens reconvened to organize a response and an investigation. Because Deputy Marshal Taylor was known to be affiliated with the gang, or "Smith crowd," he was passed over, and U.S. Commissioner C. A. Sehlbrede, as the senior official on the scene, swore in John M. Tanner as Deputy Marshal, and deputized twenty-five others to assist Tanner in rounding up the rest of the gang. Watchmen patrolled Skagway all that long night, checking in at all of the gambling joints and saloons frequented by the gang.

By the time the novice deputies searched back alleys, fenced yards, sheds, docks, and trails out of town, many of the toughs had already fled. In fact, it is most likely that many had fled even before the showdown on the wharf.

The coroner's jury convened at ten o'clock on the morning of Saturday, July 9, while the hunt for gang members continued. Shortly before five in the morning on Sunday, July 10, the Old Man, Van Tripplett was arrested after hiding out in the hills east of town where he had fled with two of the other principles of the gang, Bowers and Slim Jim Foster. Hunger had driven Tripp into town, he said, adding that he'd "rather be hung on a full stomach than die of starvation in the ____ ____ mountains."[94] About eight o'clock in the evening, Bowers, Foster, and Wilder were captured when they walked into a clearing up on the wagon road north of the cemetery, staked out by John Patten and a partner. Patten marched the three gangsters into town, arriving about midnight, and placed them all under guard at the Burkhard Hotel with Tripplett.[95]

A large mob, judged to be more than a hundred strong, had gathered in front of the hotel, anxious to lynch the prisoners, and demanding the return of Stewart's poke of gold. It fell to newly deputized Marshal Tanner to stand up to the mob and resist their entreaties for the prisoners. At three in the morning, with news of soldiers from Dyea on the way, the mob rushed the hotel. Slim Jim Foster, the youngest of the group, made a desperate leap from the rear second-floor window and fled, with the mob shooting at him. Amazingly enough, Foster was neither injured in his two-storey jump nor shot, but was captured by the mob near Bond and State Streets. Captain Tanner once again came to the fore, subdued the mob, and recovered the prisoner.

When Monday morning, July 11, dawned, twenty-seven men were in custody: twenty-three shut up in City Hall and four at the Burkhard. However, Soapy had stated that the number of gang members was 205 in his February threats, so the twenty-seven in custody were but a fraction, with most of the gang having apparently escaped without detention. The newspapers made the most of it:

> *Tripp's Philosophy*
> *What a chapter for a dime novel the adventures of Soapy Smith's Big Four on the waterworks hill would make. Hiding for two days and nights in the woods, without shelter, without food, and in nervous fear that every sound was the footstep of an avenging citizen. On Saturday Night Bowers shook Old Man Tripp crying:*
> *Wake up, wake up; they are coming to hang us.*
> *"For God's sake let me alone," said the old man, "we should have been hanged twenty years ago".*
> Daily Alaskan, *July 13, 1898*

That afternoon, a jury called numerous witnesses and carefully sifted the evidence. About 4:30, this verdict was returned, according to a souvenir booklet published by local photographers:

> *We, the jurors called to inquire into the cause of the death of Jefferson Randolph Smith, after each and all of us having examined the body of said Smith, and having heard the evidence of Dr. Cornelius and Dr. Whiting upon their medical examination of said body, and also the evidence of witnesses who were present at the death of said Smith, which took place on the Juneau Wharf, City of Skagway, District of Alaska, U.S.A., between the hours of nine and ten p.m. on July 8th, 1898, hereby find:*
> *That Smith came to his death by reason of a pistol wound piercing his heart.*
> *That said wound was the result of a pistol shot fired by one Frank H. Reid, who now lies in the* Bishop Rowe Hospital, *of Skagway, dangerously wounded from shots received at the hands of the deceased, the said Smith.*
> *That such shooting on the part of the said Reid was in self defense, and in the opinion of this jury entirely justifiable.*
> *Shea and Patten, The "Soapy" Smith Tragedy,* 1907

After visiting the prisoners on Sunday night, the Rev. Sinclair returned to his rooms to prepare for the funeral of the ignominious bandit on Monday morning, at which he had agreed to officiate. Sinclair had only recently arrived in Skagway to assist in the mission work of the Anglican Church. While it was his associate, the young R. M. Dickey, who had labored in Skagway through the winter, constructing the new church and in secret consulting with various members of the vigilante committee, in the division of labors of the new mission field, it was Sinclair who was in Skagway to witness Soapy's end. He wrote in his diary, "I was determined to give the remains a decent burial even if I should afterwards be invited to leave town because of my action."[96]

Sinclair took the precaution of asking a member of the vigilance committee to accompany the funeral procession "as a safeguard against misunderstanding and mob violence." He spent the remainder of the evening in writing out the sermon in full, "so as to forestall any misrepresentation" of what he had said.

Sinclair's diary records the events that took place Monday morning, beginning with a short service at the undertaking parlor. In addition to the minister and the undertaker, the attendees were Mr. Butler, of the vigilance committee, "three lawyers who had done business with Soapy, and a late partner of the deceased." Also present, Sinclair notes, was "his late mistress whose presence I felt was no tribute, but rather an insult to his living family in the East."

Sinclair was contemptuous of all of those citizens who had not hesitated to celebrate with Soapy in his prime, but now had not "the courage to do his remains justice." So, in the end, few were on hand to actually hear Sinclair deliver his sermon. However, he afterwards allowed it to be printed in the paper.

The existence of Soapy's mistress was apparently not much of a secret. Following the funeral, the unnamed woman attempted to leave town, but was apprehended at the docks:

> *The woman that Soapy Smith has been living with at Skagway purchased a ticket on the* City of Seattle, *and was coming to the sound. The deputy marshal boarded the boat and took her off. They afterwards allowed her to leave on the* Tartar, *but it is said, took $3,000 which she had concealed about her person.*[97]

Meanwhile, on Monday afternoon the fate of the men in custody was turned over to a citizens' committee. After hearing seventy-three witnesses, the citizens' committee found enough evidence to indict Triplett, Foster, Bowers, and Harry Bronson of larceny; George Wilder, J. D. Jackson, and John Clear of assault with a dangerous weapon; Chas Butler of inciting a riot; Al White of larceny; and S. S. Taylor, the marshal, of dereliction of duty. It was recommended that sixteen men "be permitted to leave town" because the committee was unable to find sufficient evidence to convict. Two were released.[98]

The committee decided to deport ten men on the steamship *Tartar*: J. Allan Hornsby, W. F. Saportas, the bartender Nate Pollack, C. S. Hussey, Bradley O'Brian, Chas Bromberg, J. Swain, J. Leary, Frank Brown, and Henry Smith. "They were accordingly marched to the wharf where after being lined up, the command hats-off was given, and the gang was photographed after which they were placed aboard the big steamer."[99] By Wednesday night five more men and one woman were also ordered deported, including William Tener, Bill O' Donell, Jim Hawkins, Mike Torpy, and Bert Markinson. Vi Torpy, the sole woman, apparently stood her ground and refused deportation. The paper noted that all of those deported must have had a guilty conscience, because none of the others objected, although there was no legal way to force them to leave. In fact, they could have requested an investigation and trial.

When they reached Seattle, Saportas, and Dr. J. Allen Hornsby, identified as the editor of the *Skagway Daily Alaskan*, proclaimed their innocence, and complained that they had been railroaded.[100] At two in the afternoon, Thursday, July 14, John Bowers, W. F. Foster, and Van B. Tripplett, the three gang members accused of robbing Stewart, appeared before U.S. Commissioner Sehlbrede. Three other gang members, Henry Jackson, George Wilder, and John Clear were arraigned on charges of assault with a deadly weapon. In spite of his long association with Soapy, John Clancy was never shown to be involved in the unlawful activities of the gang. The stolen gold was found in a trunk in the back room of Soapy's saloon, minus about $600.

In its notes on a city council meeting that took place on the same day, the *Skaguay News* probably understated the extent of the political corruption in Skagway:

At a special meeting of the city council held at ten o'clock Monday morning, members J. H. Foster, Frank E. Burns, and W. F. Lokowitz tendered their resignations each of which was accepted. All the members were present except Hornsby and Spencer. After the resignations were

accepted, there was one lone member, Chairman Sperry left to make second, put before the house, and vote on a motion to adjourn.
And there you are.
Skagway News, *July 15, 1898*

While Frank Reid languished close to death in Bishop Rowe Hospital, the Rev. Sinclair officiated at Soapy Smith's funeral, in the same small frame church that Smith had helped to build. Sinclair put his thoughts on the situation into his sermon, delivered to few. He chose for his text "Good understanding getteth favor; but the way of the transgressor is hard." (Prov. 13:15)[101] "We lament that in the career of one who has lived among us there is so little that we can look back upon today as unmistakably good or heroic," said Sinclair.[102]

He noted the unusual social conditions prevalent in the mining boomtowns of the West. "It is true that especially in new and only partially organized towns, the same discrimination between the pure and honorable and those who are more or less honorable is not so sharply drawn. Many who would not be seen in South or East associating with gamblers, prostitutes or grafters will walk with such on the streets, cultivate their custom in business, or even tolerate their influence in civic affairs." He further acknowledged that "This is made even more difficult by the feeling among many that their present residence is only temporary, that they are really exiles from home merely to make a stake and that necessarily many of the maxims and customs of the home land are suspended here."

However, he did not let his audience off the hook, but admonished his readers, that "Amid such circumstances it requires extra moral courage, and extra firm faith...to choose principle at a loss of profit and purity of mind and body at a loss of popularity and pleasure."

And finally, as we think of Soapy, the Rev. Sinclair speaks to us from the days of '98, urging us to see "in his fatal career the symbol of our own lesser follies." Soapy's grave was marked with a simple wooden marker bearing only his name, age and date of death.

Sinclair subsequently visited the mortally wounded Frank Reid who finally succumbed to his injuries twelve days later on July 20. The grateful citizens of Skagway buried him with great fanfare.

Soapy was buried outside the cemetery, but for Reid there was later erected a massive stone monument bearing the inscription, "He gave his life for the honor of Skagway."

Epilogue

Jefferson Randolph "Soapy" Smith, born into a genteel southern family on November 2, 1860, in Noonan, Georgia, was only thirty-eight when he died, leaving a wife and five children in St. Louis.

In December 1898, Ed Fay (AKA John Fay) was found not guilty by reason of self-defense for the murders of Andy McGrath and Marshal Rowan.

"Rev." John Bowers and W. E. "Slim Jim" Foster were at first thought to be each sentenced to one year at San Quentin. However, the *Skagway News* of December 23 brought the news that they were being taken to Sitka to serve out their terms: Bowers, one year for larceny and six months for assault and battery; Foster, one year and $1000 fine for larceny and six months for assault and battery; Van Tripplet one year for larceny. Old man Tripp died May 16, 1901.[102]

The case against the marshal, S. S. Taylor, was never heard, as in the end there were no specific charges filed against him.

Wilder, and Madigan, alias Jackson, were convicted of attempted murder.

The case of W. E. Foster, AKA J. H. Foster, alias "Slim Jim," is the strangest of all the gang members. While the man arrested in Skagway and prosecuted in Sitka was identified as W. E. Foster, there was another Foster in Skagway, a J. H. Foster who arrived in the fall of 1897, took ownership of a saloon, and was elected to the city council. It seems that these may have been the same person. Foster was perhaps the youngest of the gang, still in his twenties in 1898. He had joined the gang in Denver while in his teens. The *Daily Alaskan* reported December 10, 1899, that President William McKinley had pardoned W. E. Foster, "Slim Jim," after he had served twelve months, as Foster was said to be dying of consumption.[103]

It is very likely that this "Slim Jim" is the same man who turned up back in Denver working with the Blonger Gang, which had assumed control of underworld operations and railroaded Soapy out of town in 1896. The man arrested as John H. Foster in the final bust of the Blonger gang in 1922 was later identified as William Elmer Mead. (Note the initials used in Skagway: W. E. Foster.) Mead was convicted of conspiracy in June 1923, and sentenced to three to ten years at Canyon City Colorado. Foster/Mead was forty-eight at the time, five-foot ten, 140 pounds, and married to a woman identified as Mrs. Katherine Mead, also known as California Kate, who attended every session of court. The couple were parents of a ten-year-old daughter and a thirteen-year-old son.

Mrs. Mead later sought pardon for her husband from the governor of Colorado. Mead went on to become one of the most notorious con men in America. Not enough research has been completed to prove that there was only one man, J. H. Foster alias William Mead, but the coincidences of identities seems to point in that direction.

Soapy Smith Chronology

1860	Jefferson Randolph Smith is born in Noonan, Georgia.
1875	The Smith family moves to Round Rock, Texas.
1878	Jeff Smith arrives in Leadville, Colorado.
1879	Jeff Smith arrives in Denver, Colorado for the
first	time.
1881, July 1	The Tabor Grand Opera House opens in Denver.
1883, March 1	Elizabeth "Baby" Doe marries silver millionaire H. A. W. Tabor in Washington, D.C.
1884, Nov. 2	"Bunco deals, robbing the miners," *Rocky Mountain News* possibly the first journalistic refer ence to Soapy in Colorado.
1886, Feb. 1	Jeff marries singer Anna Neilson, in Colorado.
April 1	Jeff opens a Mexican Legion recruiting office on Larimer Street.
June 6	Wyatt Earp deals faro at Denver's Central Saloon.
June 6	Meanwhile, frontier law officer William Barclay "Bat" Masterson (1853-1921) is dealing at the Arcade.
1887, Jan. 8	*Harper's Bazaar* features drawing of "Baby" Doe Tabor.
1889, July 29	*Colorado Rocky Mountain News* editor Arkins begins his campaign against Soapy and his follow ers.
July 30	When his wife is insulted, Soapy attempts to mur der Arkins.
Aug. 1	Soapy leaves Denver for Pocatello, Idaho.
1890, May 3	"Soapy Smith in Jail: the wily bunco man turns just one trick too many." Denver (RMN)
1891, May 1	Soapy opens the Tivoli Saloon in Denver.
Oct. 4	Soapy tears up Glasson's detective agency.
Dec. 1	There is a silver strike in the San Juan Mountains.
1892, Feb. 29	Soapy moves to Creede.

March 19	Soapy's friend Joe Simons dies in Crede.
June 1	The Sherman Silver Act is repealed in Washington, D.C.
June 5	A fire destroys Ford's Exchange but not Soapy's Orleans Club.
Oct. 15	There is a shooting at Murphy's Exchange.
Oct. 16	Soapy is involved in a "wine room" crime.
1894, March 15	The City Hall War demonstrates the corruption of the city government in Denver.
1895, March 1	Soapy tries to con President Porfirio Diaz in Mexico.
Oct. 12	Soapy is jailed in Dallas, Texas.
Dec. 12	Col. Riddle is killed in Houston.
1896, Jan. 30	Soapy arrives in Denver from St. Louis, spends the day and departs for Cripple Creek.
1897, July 22	"Jeff Smith going to the Klondyke." Reported in Denver.
Mid-August	Jeff and his lieutenants arrive in Skagway, Alaska.
September	Jeff leaves to visit family in St. Louis and to recruit cons.
Oct. 1	Soapy and Jimmy Dugan get in a fight in Seattle.
Nov. 11	Jeff Smith's Parlor in Skagway advertised in news paper.
1898, Jan. 31	Bartender Fay kills Andy McGrath and Deputy Marshal Rowan.
Feb. 6	*Seattle Post-Intelligencer* reports "a dearth of law and a famine of authority" in Skagway, and names Soapy as chief instigator.
Feb. 16	The battleship *Maine* is sunk in Havana.
Feb. 22	"Hundreds sail for Alaska," reports *San Francisco Chronicle*.
Feb. 25	Officers of the *S.S. Noyo* report conditions of law lessness at Skagway.
March	Skagway citizens form Committee of 101 to redress grievances with Soapy.
March 19	Soapy writes to President William McKinley offering the services of his Skagway Military Company to fight in Cuba.

May 1	Soapy stages a parade of his volunteers.
May 2	Thugs jailed; Soapy falsely reported to be among them in Tacoma.
May 29	Prostitute Ella Wilson is murdered in Skagway.
July 4	As Grand Marshal, Soapy leads his troops in the Fourth of July parade.
July 8	In a confrontation on the Juneau dock about 9:30p.m., Soapy is killed by civil engineer Frank Reid. An armed committee gathers to round up the rest of the gang.
July 9	As a mob calls for the lives of three ringleaders, martial law is declared and U.S. troops sum moned from Dyea.
July 15	Rev. Sinclair's funeral sermon for Soapy is print-
ed	in the *Skaguay News*.
July 20	Frank Reid dies of his wounds.

Crime in Skagway

Mounties reported eight dead bodies on the White Pass trail in a single day, February 15, 1898. Soapy's latter-day defenders have tried to claim that Skagway was not as violent as it seemed.

Among the murders attributed to Soapy's reign were those of the miner H. Bean, on the trail in the early spring, and Ella Wilson in the late spring, in addition to Marshal Rowan and Andy McGrath.

The Grand Jury empanelled in November 1898 investigated 302 cases, returning 277 as true bills, as follows:

Charge	Count
Assault with a dangerous weapon	12
Larceny	12
Grossly disturbing public peace	3
Receiving stolen goods	1
Embezzlement	1
Manslaughter	2
Assault and battery	2
Witchcraft	2
Keeping house of ill-fame	1
Attempt to bribe a U.S. official	1
Negligence in office of U.S. official	1
Violation of prohibition law and violation of International revenue law	239
Total	**277**

A comparison of the above list with even a superficial reading of the many memoirs and newspaper reports makes it clear that the list seriously understates the crime levels in Skagway during the days of the Klondike Gold Rush.

Gang Members in Skagway and Denver

> *I knew Soapy personally and was proud of it, but, as I had no money and knew enough to keep my mouth shut, I was absolutely safe.... He was a bad man, but he wasn't as bad as his gang, who would stop at nothing.*
>
> *Arthur T. Walden, A Dog Puncher on the Yukon*

How many gang members were there? Two members of the citizens' committee that investigated Soapy's death, Col. Frank Keller, "The Money King of Alaska," and Dr. Whiting, compiled a list of gang members totaling 192. Unfortunately, that list has not survived the years. Soapy himself bragged in February 1898 that there were 205. Others estimated as many as 300.

This list includes known associates of Soapy Smith in both Denver and Skagway. Most of his men posed as good citizens, wearing bowler hats, wing collars, diamond stickpins and highly polished shoes or boots. Others posed as experienced prospectors, chin whiskers and all.

Following the shooting of Soapy, twenty-six men were arrested by acting deputy marshal Josiah "Si" Tanner. Of that total, eleven were bound over to the grand jury in Sitka and accompanied there by a deputy marshal from Dyea. Nine were deported on the British steamer *Tartar*. The others were freed.

Atkins, Billy Con man.

Baggs, Charles "Doc" An ace confidence man; a smiling, soft-voiced master of disguise who often posed as a rancher, a stockman, a miner, banker, minister, or laborer depending on the circumstances. He perfected some of his tricks and disguises in Denver, Colorado. He operated there from the early 1870s to 1885 when he was forced out during a "general town cleanup." He was the inventor of the gold brick scheme, and was still operating with Clay Wilson in California in 1915. The *Rocky*

Mountain News published an extensive profile of him in 1915, calling him "king of all the confidence men" and "prince of confidence men." The article said that the General Manager of the Pinkerton detective office in Denver considered only "Canada Bill" his equal in swindling exploits. A single "trick" is said to have netted him $100,000.

Before hooking up with Soapy, Baggs acted as a steerer for Frank Tarbeaux, one of the most famous Western scalawags. Baggs made and lost several fortunes in his long career. He often adopted the same kind of backwards logic as Soapy. He once declared, "I defy the newspapers to put their hands on a single man I ever bit that wasn't financially able to stand it. I am emotionally insane. When I see anyone looking in a jewelry store thinking how they would like to get away with the diamonds, an irresistible desire comes over me to skin them. I don't drink, smoke, chew or cheat poor people; I pay my debts." At the age of 93, in 1930, Baggs was living on an estate near New York City.

Bowers, "Reverend" Charles a gifted steerer who sometimes posed as a man of the cloth, Bowers was given the job of engaging prosperous-looking cheechakos (the Chinook word for newcomers) in conversation and warning them of the pitfalls of Skagway. He'd tell them where the "trustworthy" gambling houses were located. Soapy met Bowers in Denver. He was one of the few gang members to be photographed in Skagway. Bowers was arrested in Skagway after Soapy's shootout with Reid.

Dog musher Arthur Walden reports in his autobiography that Bowers was quick to hit people over the head and have them thrown into the street when he disliked their behavior. After he killed a deputy sheriff and the man fell on his face, Bowers rolled him over. Recognizing him, he said, "I've killed the sheriff. Ain't that too bad!" (*A Dog Puncher on the Yukon*, p. 133)

Bromley or Bromberg, Charles Arrested in Skagway, deported.

Bronson, Harry L. Arrested in Skagway.

Brooks, "Dolly," also known as **"The Duke of Halstead Street."**

Brown, Frank Arrested in Skagway, deported.

Bruce, Jimmy, "The Great Gobblefish" Loan shark.

Bull, John Capped for Canada Bill on trains out of Omaha. "John Bull" is the British equivalent of "the average man," so this may well be a pseudonym.

Burns, Big Ed A heavy or strong-arm man; a person employed to use violence or coercion. Burns followed Soapy to Skagway. One of his chores was to follow Soapy about town and ward off beggars so he could choose those to whom he showed his "high-handed benevolence." Soapy was chivalrous toward certain people, such as widows and orphans stranded at Skagway by the deaths of prospectors in the Klondike.

Butler, Charles Arrested in Skagway.

Cady, "Troublesome Tom" A thimble-rig and gunman, associated with Soapy in both Denver and the silver boomtown of Creede. He also worked with Doc Baggs in Cheyenne, Wyoming.

Canada Bill or William Jones A cardsharp and trickster more than a confidence man. He earned his stripes in Chicago and Omaha, and was known for swindling passengers aboard the Union Pacific and Kansas Pacific Railroads. He specialized in three-card monte, a modified form of faro. He was part of Soapy's gang in Denver.

Canada Bill once wrote to the general superintendent of the Union Pacific offering $25,000 a year for the exclusive rights to run a three-card monte game on the trains' passenger cars. He promised to limit his victims to commercial travelers from Chicago and Methodist preachers. The railroad declined. One of Bill's favorite sayings was, "Suckers have no business with money, anyway."

Chase, Big Ed Owner of the Palace and Arcade in Denver.

Clear, John Arrested in Skagway.

Conlin, Claude Alexander A mark who was taken for every penny he had in Soapy's shell game. Soapy took pity on him and made him a member of the Skagway gang, in charge of prostitute management. He later became a vaudeville star as a psychic, "Alexander, the Man Who Knows."

Cripen, Tom

Daugherty, William

Dixon, Syd A steerer and shill. Dixon, who had become a dope addict, was the black sheep of a prominent eastern family. He was a disbarred lawyer capable of giving Soapy legal advice.

Dugronder, F.J. Arrested in Skagway.

Edwards, Henry or "Yank Hank Fewclothes" Steerer. A poet who peddled honey on the streets of Denver when he was not working a con. His nickname derived from the fact that he never wore a coat, vest or overcoat even in cold weather until Soapy made him change his ways.

Fielding, William Gang member in Skagway. Captured at Sheep Camp, one of the stops on the Chilkoot Trail where prospectors paused overnight.

Foster, "Slim Jim," J.H., or **W.F. or W.E.** Shill, also known as Elmer Mead. After the duel between Soapy and Frank Reid on July 8, 1898, several gang members including Foster hid in the woods. They surrendered after two days. Skagway's citizens wanted to hang the gang, but they were prevented. Foster was arrested and served one year in jail at Sitka. Eighteen months after Soapy's death, Foster was pardoned by President McKinley because he was said to be dying of consumption.

Gaylord, Ed Saloon owner in Denver.

Gibbs, Red See Red below.

Gray or Grey, Fatty A heavy.

Green, Fatty Also known as "Shoot Your Eyes Out" Green, like Big Ed, was a strong-arm man. He dealt with customers who protested they had been cheated, often by murdering them.

Harris, Frisco Red Heavy. See Red below.

Hawkins, John Arrested in Skagway, deported.

Hopkins, Yeah Mow A strong-arm man who learned his craft in San Francisco's Chinatown where he served as a bodyguard to wealthy Chinese during the Tong wars. He was known for his ability to "soften up" suckers. He took part in a Skagway swindle that involved receiving "letters."

Hornsby, J. Allen Arrested in Skagway and deported.

Hussey, C.L. Arrested in Skagway and deported.

Jackson, T. Arrested in Skagway. Following Soapy's death and their arrest, Jackson, Bowers, Foster, Wilder, Old Man Tripp and ex-Marshal Taylor were indicted by a grand jury, brought to trial and given sentences in federal prison ranging from one to ten years.

Jackson, W.H. His artistic talents made him skilled at creating false-fronts.

Jones, William See "Canada Bill."

Kelly, "Rincon Kid" Skin game artist; perhaps got his nickname from the town of Rincon, Georgia.

Kid, Jimmy Fresh A new thug who joined the gang in Skagway.

King of Terrors One of many "lambs" who managed to escape the clutches of the law in Skagway.

Kingsley, R. Arrested in Skagway.

Leary, J.A. Arrested in Skagway, deported.

Light, John Gun fighter.

Markinson, Bert Arrested in Skagway, deported.

Mizner, Wilson (1876-1933) Extortionist, bootlegger, murderer, wit and playwright. One of his schemes in Skagway was working as a dust weigher in a dance hall. While balancing the scales, he would contrive to tip a bit of dust onto a small carpet. At the end of each week, he would burn the carpet and extract the gold from its ashes. After Skagway, Mizner went on to Dawson and Nome where he managed fighters. Irving Berlin tried to write a musical based on his life.

Moon Faced Kid New thug who joined the gang in Skagway. He may be the model for the protagonist of Jack London's story "Moon Face."

Murphy, "Ice Box" Safecracker, Denver.

Murphy, John Owned the Exchange Saloon; served two years of a six-year sentence for killing his wife.

Nieman, James H. Arrested in Skagway.

O'Brien, Bradley Arrested in Skagway, deported.

O'Donnell, Billy Arrested in Skagway, deported.

Palmer, Joe Lieutenant in Creede.

Parker, Banjo A heavy in Denver.

Pollock, Nate The nattily-dressed bartender at Soapy's saloon in Skagway. Arrested and deported after Soapy's death.

"Red" Little is known about him; he appears in a photo of Soapy in his saloon with Nate Pollock, John Bowers, John Clancy and the Sheeney Kid. See Frisco Red Harris and Red Gibbs.

Saportas, W.F. or Billy Reporter, steerer. Saportas came to Alaska as a New York newspaper correspondent. Soapy put him to work for *The Alaskan*, whose editor was on Smith's payroll. Saportas would "interview" newcomers at the docks, helping them carry their baggage into town and finding out if they had enough money on them to be worthwhile targets. He was arrested in Skagway, put aboard the *Tartar* and told not to return. He may be the same man as the Fred Saportas who was a track and field champion in 1876 as a member of the Harlem Athletic Club; his specialty was the 100-yard dash.

Simons, Joe Soapy's friend who died of pneumonia in Creede.

Sheeney Kid Gang member in Skagway.

Slim, Jay Bird

Smith, Bascom or Bascomb Soapy's brother; a lieutenant in Creede, active in Denver. As of October 1895, he was in jail in connection with the assault made upon John J. Hughes.

Smith, Henry Arrested in Skagway, deported.

Swaim or Swain, J.A. Arrested in Skagway, deported.

Torpy, M.J. Arrested in Skagway, deported.

Torpy, Vi Wife of M.J. Torpy. Arrested in Skagway, refused to be deported.

Tener, William Arrested in Skagway.

The Blackjack Heavy, new thug who joined in Skagway.

The Lamb New thug who joined the gang in Skagway.

The Queen A new thug who joined in Skagway.

Thornton, Jimmy A thug who was part of the Denver gang.

Tripplett or **Tripplet, Van B.** or **"Old Man Tripp"** One of the original con men, partner of George Devol. He worked the trails out of town, posing as a sourdough full of information about the Klondike. With his long white hair and kindly manner, he easily conned new arrivals. Triplett was arrested in Skagway and still in jail when Foster was pardoned. He died May 16, 1901.

Van Horn, Judge Steerer in Denver and Skagway.

Warman, Cy Editor in Creede.

White, A.L. Arrested in Skagway.

Wilder, George Businessman, authority on investment opportunities who directed affluent prospectors to "a sure thing." He operated in Denver where he was arrested for steering a newcomer into a poker game where the man lost all his money. Arrested in Skagway.

Wilson, Clay Con who killed Jim Moon in Denver; worked with Doc Baggs. Died in 1915.

Endnotes

List of Abbreviations

CHS	*Colorado Historical Society*
DN	*Denver News*
DP	*Denver Post*
DR	*Denver Republican*
DT	*Denver Times*
DPL	Denver Public Library, Western History Collection
EAB/DPL	E. A. Burton Collection, Denver Public Library
KLGC	Klondike Gold Rush National Park, Archives, Skagway
RMN	*Rocky Mountain News*
SN	*Skaguay News*
UAF	University of Alaska Fairbanks, Archives

1 The story about Reliable packers appears in Frank G. Robertson and Beth Kay Harris. *Soapy Smith: King of the Frontier Con Men.* New York: Hastings House Publishers, 1961, p. 178-179; and is repeated in Pierre Berton's *Klondike Fever.*, p. 163.

2 As far as I have been able to determine, all of the gang members were indeed men.

3 "J.Smith of Leadville, hotel guest" RMN 03/05/1879 p4c2; Citations to Denver Newspapers, from the E.A. Burton Collection at the Denver Public Library. [hereafter EAB/DPL] Other similar articles are in the Dawson Scrapbooks at the Colorado Historical Society, particularly volume 20.

4 W.P. Carstenphen, letter to the editor following Barnacle's article, *The Trail*, Jan. 1920; DPL

5 George Tower Buffam, *Smith of Bear City.* New York, The Grafton Press, 1906. (DPL) p26-30.

6 Buffam, *Smith of Bear City.* ibid.

7 Karen R. Thompson, and Jane H DiGesualdo,. *Historical Round Rock, Texas.* Austin, TX: Eakin Press, 1985. p. 275. Thanks to Austin History Center, Austin Texas.

8 Carstenphen letter, *The Trail*, June 1920

9 Barkalow Barnacle, article, *The Trail*, Jan. 1920; p. 5-11. From an interview Barnacle conducted with Co. Edwin "Bobo" Smith. DPL

10 There is no actual documentation of this cowboying story, although it is frequently repeated. [see Robert K. DeArment, *Knights of the Green Cloth.* Norman: University of Oklahoma Press, 1982. p. 364.]

It's difficult to imagine the slick and fastidious Soapy actually doing the hard work required of even a junior cowboy on the long cattle trail. The cowboy story may be just an attempt to include the popular cowboy mythology associated with Texas and the west with Soapy's story. However, it is likely that Soapy first came across Hall and the shell game in association with a circus.

11 Maurer, David. *The Big Con.* New York, Bobbs-Merrill, 1940

12 Maurer, David. "The Argot of the Three Shell Game," in *The Language of the Underworld.* Collected and Edited by Allan W. Futrell and Charles Wordell. Lexington, University Press of Kentucky, 1981. pp. 162-172.

13 Phyllis Flanders Dorset, *The New Eldorado,* New York: The Macmillan Co., 1970.

14 "J.Smith of Leadville, hotel guest" RMN 03/05/1879 p4c2;

15 RMN EAB/DPL March 1, 1882, p. 5, column 1.

16 William Ross Collier and Edwin Victor Westrate, *The Reign of Soapy Smith, Monarch of Misrule.* Garden City, New York: The Sun Dial Press, pp. 28-29.

17 Obituary of Ed Chase, *Denver Post,* Sept. 28, 1921, Dawson Scrapbook, CHS, Vol. 20, p. 67.

18 "Gambling and tragedy at once famous Arcade," *Rocky Mountain News,* July 11, 1915. Mongold scrapbook, DPL, p. 108 and following. This was one in a series of articles on the old, wide-open Denver, published on the occasion of the beginning of Prohibition. Carstenphen letter, *The Trail,* June, 1920.

19 Carstenphen letter, *The Trail,* June, 1920.

20 DeArment, *Knights of the Green Cloth,* p. 113

21 DeArment, *Knights*: p. 164. Clark Secrest: *Hell's Belles: Denver's Brides of the Multitudes.* Aurora, Colorado: Hindsight Historical Publications, 1996. p. 129.

22 Secrest. *Hell's Belles,* p. 135

23 Howard Clifford, *Uncrowned King of Skagway.* Seattle: Sourdough Enterprise, 1997.

24 Collier and Westrate, *The Reign of Soapy Smith,* pp. 28-29.

25 McKeown, *The Trail Led North,* p. 112.

26 Maurer, *The Big Con* p. 1

27 Ibid.

28 DeArment, *Knights,* p. 308, quoting Maurer, *The Big Con.*

29 *Rocky Mountain News,* EAB/DPL, various articles.

30 Maurer, *Language of the Underworld.*

31 Maurer, *The Big Con,* pp. 17-18.

32 "Doc Baggs, King of the Confidence Men," *Denver News,* Aug. 8, 1915, DPL Mongold Collection.

33 The motion picture *The Sting* supplies an example, taken from incidents and characters in Maurer's book, *The Big Con.*

34 "Doc Baggs". Ibid.
35 Ibid.
36 Ibid.
37 DPL Mongold Collection Scrapbook, p. 104. Probably from the Denver News, Aug. 8, 1915
38 EAB/DPL: *RMN*, Jan. 31, 1879.
39 EAB/DPL: "Mrs. Charles watch stolen by thief." *RMN*, May 29, 1880.
40 *Denver Republican*, July 27, 1892.
41 Robertson and Harris, p. 46. See also *The Brand Book of the Westerners*, September, 1951. DPL.
42 Foster, whose real name was probably William Mead, played the role of an eager shill who drummed up business for the street and parlor games. It is possible that he is the same man as the J. H. Foster who was still involved in bunco games in Denver twenty-five years later when he was arrested with the Blonger gang. Colorado Court records, 1923.
43 Dorset, *The New Eldorado*, p. 322.
44 Davis, *Harper's Monthly*, quoted in Dorset, *The New Eldorado*, p. 323.
45 *Rocky Mountain News*, July 29, 1889; quoted in DeArment, *Knights*, p. 368, and Robertson and Harris, p. 73.
46 Citations are from the E. A. Burton Collection, RMN Index, DPL.
47 Collier and Westrate, p. 145.
48 "Gossip from Creede," *Colorado Sun*, Denver, Feb. 15, 1892, quoted in Nolie Mumey, *Creede: The History of a Colorado Silver Mining Town*, Denver, Artcraft Co., 1949, p. 100, quoted in Dorset, p. 325.
49 Millard Everette in the *Denver Catholic Register*. Series of Articles, beginning March 20, 19p. 100. CHS
50 EAB/DPL, *Rocky Mountain News*, index; dates as noted.
51 "A Sucker refuses to play..." *Denver Republican*, July 27, 1892.
52 Collier and Westrate, p. 164.
53 Dorset. *Eldorado*, pp. 342-343
54 Phillip Van Cise, *Fighting the Underworld*, New York, Houghton Mifflin, 1936, p. 213.
55 Collier and Westrate, p. 183.
56 Collier and Westrate place the Mexican adventure in early 1896. Others place it in 1895, or even 1894. Jose de la Cruz Porfirio Diaz (1830-1915) served two terms as president of Mexico, 1877-80 and 1884-1911.
57 Robertson and Harris, p. 163. date of original clipping unknown.
58 Robertson and Harris, p. 163-64, attributed to "*another paper in Denver.*"
59 *Denver Times*, July 22, 1897.
60 Howard Clifford, *The Skagway Story*, p. 10.
61 *Washington Evening Star*, Oct. 13, 1897, collection of A. H. Brooks, UAF; from KLGC.

62 *New York World*, Sept. 17, 1897.

63 These letters were first published in a two-part article in the *Alaska Yukon Magazine*, edited by R. D. Jones: "Correspondence of a Crook," January 1907 and February 1908. The magazine said that the original scrapbook was "found in the bottom of a trunk," and then later retrieved from the dust-covered archives of the Sheriff's library in Skagway. After the first publication of the correspondence, neither the scrapbook nor the actual letters were ever seen again. The letters have been reprinted most recently as *Correspondence of a Crook*, edited by Howard Clifford.

64 Shea and Patton, *The Soapy Smith Tragedy*, 1907, unpaged.

65 For the rest of Molly's story, see Art Peterson and C. Scott Williams, *Murder, Madness and Mystery: An Historical Narrative of Mollie Walsh*; Clifford, *The Skagway Story*, and Claire Rudolph Murphy and Jane G. Haigh, *Gold Rush Women*.

66 T. Fischer. *In Search of Eldorado*, 1905. Quoted in Pierre Berton, *Klondike Fever*, p. 160.

67 The story about Saportas appears in Robertson and Harris, *Soapy Smith*, p. 205.

68 *Seattle Post-Intelligencer*, Feb. 25, 1898.

69 While a primary source for early Skagway history and Soapy's escapades in Skagway is the *Skaguay News*, the editions of Feb. 3 and Feb. 11, 1898, are missing, as are many numbers of that year.

70 *Seattle Post-Intelligencer*, Feb. 6, 1898.

71 Note that the article states the events took place when Soapy "returned in the winter." This corroborates the evidence that he did in fact visit St. Louis and Seattle, but made his way back to Skagway some time before the McGrath and Rowan murders.

72 Clifford, *Uncrowned*, p. 93.

73 *Seattle Post-Intelligencer*. Dr. Rufus Smith mentioned in *San Francisco Chronicle*, Feb. 11, 1898, p. 2.

74 *San Francisco Chronicle* Feb. 14, 1898, p5c2.

75 *San Francisco Chronicle* Feb. 8, 1898, p2c3.

76 *Seattle Post-Intelligencer* Feb. 12, 1898.

77 *Seattle Post-Intelligencer*, various issues, February 1898. News of the incident in front of the Whitehorse Saloon reached Seattle on February 22.

78 R. M. Dickey, edited by Art Peterson. *Gold Fever: A Narrative of the Great Klondike Gold Rush*. Auke Bay: Klondike Research, 1997, p. 18-19.

79 The last item in Soapy's scrapbook, published in *Alaska Yukon Magazine*, "Correspondence of a Crook," is an article clipped from the *San Francisco Examiner* of March 16, 1898, "Troops Rule at Skagway," datelined Victoria, March 15.

80 According to C. L. Andrews, perhaps the first to thoroughly investigate the Soapy Smith story, it is probable that Soapy wrote the warning himself. Andrews says, "...the exact dates of these meetings and bulletins, while not on record, was about March 1898."

81 McKeown, p. 104.

82 This incident is from Robertson and Harris, p. 188, and Clifford, *Uncrowned*, p. 88.

83 Howard Clifford, *Uncrowned*, p. 90. See also Velma Lung, *Black Sand and Gold.*

84 Letters from the Howard Clifford Collection reprinted in *Uncrowned King*. Harry L. Suydam, "The Reign of Soapy Smith," *Frank Leslie's Popular Monthly*, January 1901; *Seattle Post-Intelligencer* May 9, 1898.

85 Secrest, *Hell's Belles*, p. 235, cf. Parkhill, *The Wildest of the West*

86 Howard Clifford, *Uncrowned*, p. 86; *San Francisco Chronicle*, June 4, 1898, p. 4, dateline Skagway, May 29.

87 *Skagway News*, July 15, 1898.

88 *Daily Alaskan*, July 2, 1898, and Frank J. Clancy, "I was Just a Kid," *Alaska Sportsman*, October 1955, pp. 16-18, 25.

89 Clancy, ibid.

90 *Skaguay News* July 8, 1898.

91 Clifford, *The Skagway Story*, pp. 10-11.

92 *Daily Alaskan*, July 11, 1898, 10 a.m. EXTRA, p. 1.

93 *The Skaguay News*, July 15, 1898.

94 James M. Sinclair, *Mission: Klondike*. Based on the diaries of John A. Sinclair.

95 *Seattle Post-Intelligencer*, July 17, 1898, p. 10, column 1. Also mentioned in *Daily Alaskan* EXTRA, July 11, 1898, p. 1.

96 *Skaguay News* July 15, 1898, quoting the report of the committee issued July 11, 1898.

97 *Skaguay News* July 15, 1898, p. 2.

98 *Seattle Post-Intelligencer*, July 17, 1898, p. 9.

99 Sinclair, *Mission: Klondike*, Canada, Mitchell Press, 1978.

100 *Daily Alaskan.*

101 Colorado District Court Case No. 26874.

Glossary of Confidence Terms

Big store An elaborate fake business establishment put together specifically as a stage for a bunco or con game.

Bucking the tiger Challenging the faro tables; the tiger frequently appeared on the faro cards and became a universal symbol for faro.

Bunco steerer A person employed as a decoy in a swindle. (*Webster's International Dictionary*, 1893)

Bunco, bunco game Webster's International Dictionary, 1893, a type of game involving cards, or a kind of swindling game or scheme, by means of cards, or a lottery sham.

Capper A decoy, a shill, often a fake winner at the shell game. The term came into use in English slang about 1580. (*Random House Webster's College Dictionary*, 1991)

Con game Short for confidence game.

Confidence game An elaborate swindle based on winning the confidence of the intended victim.

Confidence man The practitioner of a swindle, usually involving several partners working a prepared script.

Faro Faro was one of the most popular card games of the American West. It was first played in France, and from there, adopted by the English nobility, leading many to bankruptcy. Faro is played against the house. The dealer deals two cards at a time from a card case, the first a losing card, and the second the winner. Bets are placed on each turn. It is named for the picture of an Egyptian pharaoh on the original decks.

Grift The practice of professional crime, requiring intelligence and thought as well as the ability to improvise to suit the moment.

Grifter One who engages in swindles and cheating, or "one who lives by his wits."

Grip man, Glad hander An individual who knows all of the closely guarded handshakes of various fraternal orders and secret societies, and uses them to greet suckers, and steer them to the games of the gang.

Heavy The tough gang member who dispenses violent punishment and protects the gangleader.

Keister Old English for suitcase, or satchel; the container for the dried pea and shells used in the shell game and, probably, for any profits.

Keno An early form of the game of bingo, first seen in New Orleans.

Mark The victim picked out for a confidence game.

Monte, or Spanish Monte A Spanish card game containing many elements of faro, and played with a forty-card Spanish deck. Spanish monte was encountered by American travelers in the Mexican influences southwest and California.

Plunger A high-stakes player willing to wager a large amount.

Shell game The original and simplest confidence game, involving three walnut shells and a pea. The operator hides the pea under one shell, and invites the crowd to guess which one as he dexterously shuffles the shells.

Shill One who poses as a satisfied customer or an enthusiastic gambler to dupe bystanders into participating in a swindle. (*American Heritage Dictionary*).

Steerer The outside man who ropes in the mark in a confidence game.

Stick A supporting or bit player in the more elaborate bunco games.

Sting A complicated confidence game planned and executed with great care, especially an operation organized and implemented by undercover agents to apprehend criminals. (*American Heritage Dictionary*)

Sucker The victim of the confidence game, or "one who is easily deceived, a dupe." (*American Heritage Dictionary*)

Thimble rig Another name for the shell game, refers to the original game using thimbles.

Three-card monte A crooked confidence game similar to the shell game, but using three cards, not to be confused with monte, or Spanish monte. A game in which a bettor must identify a stipulated card from among three cards after they have been moved around facedown on the table. The game came into American popularity about 1890. (*Random House Webster's*

College Dictionary). See also monte/Spanish monte.

Thug A violent gangster or gang member, synonym of "heavy."

Tong An association or a secret society of Chinese in the United States, believed to be involved in organized crime. (*American Heritage Dictionary*)

Tripe According to one theory, tripe was slang for something worthless, in this case the soap. Another theory defines tripe as short for tripod or the stand for the case: tripe and keister is the satchel full of goods, or the tripod and the case.

Bibliography

Web Sites
www.explorenorth.com
www.nps.gov/klgo/
www.skagway.com
www.soapysmith.net
www.faroking.com

Books and Articles

Barnacle, Barkalow. (untitled article) *The Trail.* Jan. 1920. DPL

Buffam, George Tower. *Smith of Bear City.* New York: The Grafton Press, 1906

Burke,John. *The Legend of Baby Doe.* Lincoln: University of Nebraska Press,1974.

Churchill, E. Richard. *Doc Holliday, Bat Masterson and Wyatt Earp: their Colorado Careers.*

Clifford, Howard, editor. *Correspondence of a Crook.* Seattle, Washington: Sourdough Enterprises, 1997.

———. *The Skagway Story.* 1975. Reprint, Whitehorse, Yukon Territory, Canada: Wolf Creek Books, 2003.

———. *Uncrowned King of Skagway.* Seattle: Sourdough Enterprises, 1997.

———. *Wyatt Earp and Friends: Alaska Adventures.* Seattle: Sourdough Enterprises, 2000.

Collier, William Ross, and Edwin Victor Westrate. *The Reign of Soapy Smith, Monarch of Misrule.* Garden City, New York: The Sun Dial Press, 1937.

Davis-Clyde, Brion. *Something for Nothing: The Lore and Lure of Gambling.* Philadelphia: Lippencott, 1956.

Davis, Richard Harding. *The West through a Car Window.* New York: Harper and Brothers, 1892.

DeArment, Robert K. *Knights of the Green Cloth.* Norman: University of Oklahoma Press, 1982.

———. *Bat Masterson: the Man and the Legend.* Norman: University of Oklahoma Press, 1979.

Dickey, R. M. *Gold Fever: A Narrative of the Great Klondike Gold Rush.* edited by Art Peterson. Auke Bay: Klondike Research, 1997.

Dorset, Phyllis Flanders. *The New Eldorado.* New York: The Macmillan Co.,1970.

Findlay, John M. *People of Chance: Gambling in American Society, From Jamestown to Las Vegas.* New York: Oxford University Press, 1986.

Fowler, Gene. *Timberline*. New York: Covici Friede Publishers, 1933.
Gill, John A. "*Miner's Diary, Goldrush 1898-1899, Dawson City.*" Diary transcribed by Henry Boulton. 1998. (on website)..
Maurer, David. *The Big Con*. New York, Bobbs-Merrill, 1940.
———. "*The Argot of the Three Shell Game.*" *Language of the Underworld*. Collected and edited by Allan W. Futrell and Charles Wordell. Lexington, Kentucky: The University Press of Kentucky (1981): 162-172.
Mumey, Nolie. *Creede: The History of a Colorado Silver Mining Town*. Denver, Colorado: Artcraft Co., 1949.
Murphy, Claire Rudolph, and Jane G. Haigh. *Gold Rush Women*. Portland: Alaska Northwest Books, 1998.
Nathan, George Jean. "*The old time train gambler.*" Harper's Weekly (May 21, 1910)
Parkhill, Forbes. *The Wildest of the West*. New York: Henry Holt and Co., 1951.
Peterson, Art, and C. Scott Williams. *Murder, Madness and Mystery: An Historical Narrative of Mollie Walsh Bartlett*. Williams, Oregon: Castle Peak Editions, 1991.
Pullen, Harriet S. *Soapy Smith: Bandit of Skagway; How He Lived; How He Died*. Skagway: Skagway Tourist Agency. No date. Collection of Lloyd "Kinky" Bayers, Alaska State Library, Juneau.
Robertson, Frank G., and Beth Kay Harris. *Soapy Smith: King of the Frontier Con Men*. New York: Hastings House Publishers, 1961.
Secrest, Clark. *Hell's Belles: Denver's Brides of the Multitudes*. Aurora, Colorado: Hindsight Historical Publications, 1996.
Sinclair, James M. *Mission: Klondike*. Canada: Mitchell Press, 1978.
Steffa, Don. "*Soapy Smith: Bad Man and Bluffer.*" Pacific Monthly, (October, 1908): .
Teacher, Lawrence, and Richard E. Nicholls, eds. *The Unabridged Jack London*. Philadelphia: Courage Books, 1997.
Time-Life Books. *The Gamblers*. Alexandria, Virginia: Time-Life Books, 1978.
Van Cise, Philip S. *Fighting the Underworld*. Cambridge, Ma.: Riverside Press; 1936.
Walden, Arthur T. A *Dog Puncher on the Yukon*. 1928. Reprint, Whitehorse, Yukon, Canada: Wolf Creek Books.
Wilson, Graham. *The White Pass and Yukon Route Railway*. Whitehorse: Wolf Creek Books.

Index

Jane Haigh

Jane Haigh lives in Fairbanks, where she researches and writes about Alaska history. Jane and Claire Rudolf Murphy have co-authored *Gold Rush Women*, *Children of the Gold Rush* and *Gold Rush Dogs*. Jane has also published two photo histories: *Denali: Early Photographs of Our National Parks* and *The Alaska Highway, A Historic Photographic Journey.*

Soapy's adventures were so interesting, that Jane has made Con Men in Denver the focus of her Dissertation for the Phd. in U.S. History at the University of Arizona in Tucson.

Fascinating Related Books

The Skagway Story

Howard Clifford
ISBN: 0-9732683-4-4
Skagway was the Carson City of the North. Its past as a rip roaring gold rush town is captured in this little scrapbook-like volume.

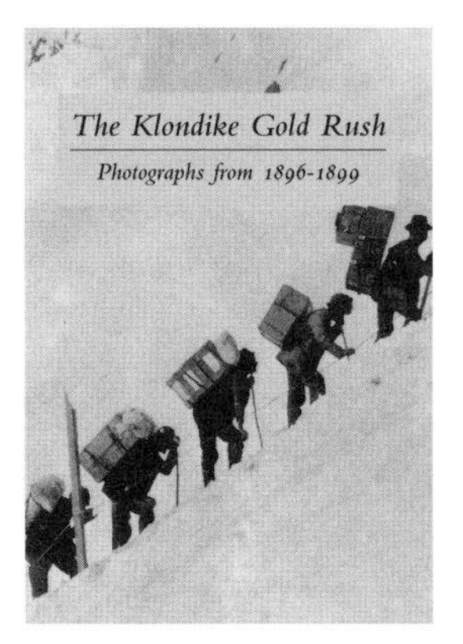

The Klondike Gold Rush Photographs from 1896-1899

Graham Wilson
ISBN 0-9681955-0-4
This best-selling collection of 125 archival photographs documents the Klondike Gold Rush and tells the day-to-day story of the ordinary stampeder. Carefully selected anecdotes and written accounts provide further insights on this fascinating event

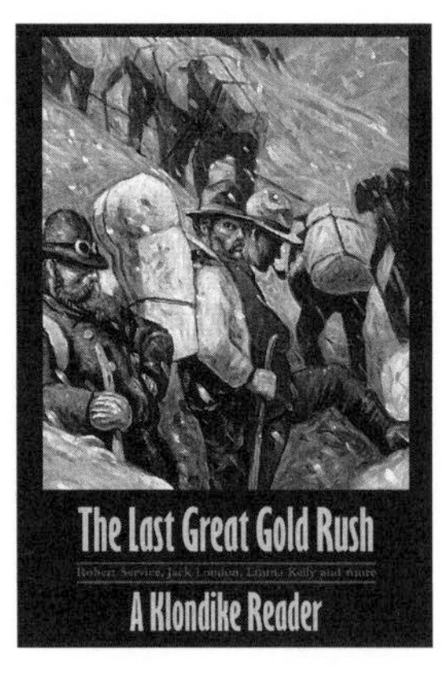

The Last Great Gold Rush A Klondike Reader

Graham Wilson (ed.)
ISBN: 0-9687091-2-5
This collection records the epic Klondike adventure at its gripping best. This anthology of historical writing is an honest portrait by famous writers as well as ordinary stampeders including Robert Service, William Ogilvie, Jack London, Tappan Adney, and many others.